THE AUOTGRAPH

The birth of a premature, frail baby girl secretly given up for adoption, followed by the mysterious death of the mother, a famous movie star, will begin a devastating chain reaction that will echo into the next two generations.

There's only one person, the housekeeper that knows the secrets.

Lives will change and so will Major League baseball.

By Ron Kattawar

Acknowledgements

Without the editorial and publishing expertise of our wonderful daughter, Kim Kattawar Mahfouz, I would be lost. Kim keeps me on track.

Danny Thomas is a Giddy-up friend. One of those rare friends that doesn’t ask questions but tackles whatever I ask of him. I call him my “eagle eye.” Danny edits like no other can. All I have to do is ask and he always replies, “Giddy-up.”

Carol, my wife, is patient and understanding. A writer always goes absent for a time, living in a world that is created for each story. With my ambitious goal of publishing a book in each month in 2015, it’s also a test to her patience and understanding. Twelve in twelve. It’s a tough goal and I’ll need a bit more of her patience than usual.

Dedications

This book is dedicated to Mary Showah. She is the template of a strong woman and gave me direction and focus from her example. She backed away from no one and never compromised her position.

Growing up and witnessing her strength I could have never developed Beth, the main character in "The Autograph."

Mary Showah, a strong woman decades ahead of her time. She has no more battles to fight. Rest well.

Isbn 13:978 1508447115
Isbn – 10:150844711X
Version 1.0

Table of Contents

CHAPTER ONE

The rain fell and no one seemed to care. I sat for what seemed an eternity, looking out the window at the dreary weather. Her cheap rocker squeaked every time I made the slightest move. Everything was as if it were slow motion. Nothing felt real. Last night this house was alive, and so was the famous owner.

As I sat and watched the rain slide down the panes, I wondered what happened. She was fine near midnight. It was the last time we talked. She was animated and full of life. She talked of her Joey, endlessly. Although they were divorced, they spent a lot of time together. He never knew. I couldn't tell him. It would break his heart if he knew everything. He was too fine a man for me to tell her vile secret to. I will never understand why she did the things she did, especially that stormy night four years ago.

I was just a housekeeper, maybe sometimes a friend. I never pretended to be a friend, but sometimes she would call me in as she lay there in her silk gown. She wanted company. She wanted someone to talk to. At those times, I was more of a friend at her convenience than a hired servant. I don't especially like that word, servant, but in my case it surely fit. Make no mistake, I was a servant.

She complained about so many people wanting so much from her, even if she wasn't making a movie or had weeks and months of appearances. In the next breath she complained because she was alone. Sometimes I could hear her talking, and I thought she had a visitor, only to find out later she was alone.

I remember the first bath she asked me to draw for her. It had to be piping hot. Next to her tub was a small refrigerator, specially installed. She would open the door to the small refrigerator at bath time, and take out five clear bottles of ice-cold milk and pour it into her steamy bath, followed by two bottles of calamine lotion. She swore by that formula and never missed a night. Last night was no different. By ten she was ready for her bath, so as usual, I drew it as hot as it would flow. I stood and watched as she poured. She would sit on the bathroom floor in bra and panties, reaching over to stir the hot water while swirling in the ice-cold milk. When she was ready for the calamine lotion, she began pouring at the foot of the tub, and by the time she reached the head, the calamine bottle was empty. Then she started at the head of the tub with the second bottle, and by the time she got to the foot, it was empty. It was as if she knew exactly when to start pouring and exactly when she would run out. I watched her perform this ritual every night for nine years.

After soaking for exactly forty-five minutes, she required a martini, dry. Actually, she demanded very dry, with five lime slices. That woman would eat the five limes, peel and all, as she sipped her drink.

I never asked why she did those things, or other bizarre things. I figured she was paying me and anything that happened was none of my business. She made me sign a legal form swearing that I would not divulge any of her secrets. I signed the form when I went to work for her, and frankly I never thought much of telling anything about her, until now – now that she is dead. She swore the milk and calamine kept her skin soft and supple. The limes she believed, kept weight off. Maybe that's true, maybe not. It doesn't matter because she believed it.

As I glanced around her bedroom and away from the dreary weather outside her bedroom window, I could see her things. She didn't have a strong desire to collect stuff, well, except clothes. She loved clothes. Mostly the items in her bedroom were gifts. Very expensive gifts, but certainly not anything she would buy for herself. She really was selective frugal. When she bought her bedroom set, it was cheap, fake lamented maple. Pretty when new, but in this California heat, the glue didn't stick for long.

Her bed was always covered with expensive sheets and pillowcases. She told me once her pillows cost over one hundred dollars each. She paid more for her pillows than she did for the bedroom set. She loved the feel of expensive fabric close to her, but beyond that, if it didn't touch her body, she always bought bottom line. My mother would have said she was cheap. Maybe she was on most things, unless like I said, it was touching her skin. Clothes - my, oh, my - that woman spent a fortune on clothes!

When she undressed for her bath every night, part of her ritual was to once again have me promise that I would burn her panties and bra. She never wore them twice. Her cheap dresser was full of expensive underwear. She never slept in anything but a sheer, see through, silk gown, no panties. I saw some panties with the price tag still on them. After I got her to sleep one night and I was alone in my bare, small bedroom I added up what she paid for one pair of panties times thirty days a month. She paid more for her panties every month than she paid me.

Now; there she is crooked across her bed, dead. She was young, beautiful, wealthy beyond imagination, and no longer breathing. I slipped a pair of panties on her. They wouldn't like it if they knew I moved her, but I had too much respect for her to let her be taken to the morgue unladylike.

I swear I am glad we didn't need an ambulance in a hurry. Her being dead and all, it wasn't like an emergency, but still it seemed like it took hours. I would have to clean up the breakfast tray I dropped when I found her. She didn't appear to be asleep. I knew she was dead the second I laid eyes on her. No person alive could look like she did, even as beautiful as she was. I just hope they catch the people who did this to her.

Finally, the ambulance arrived, and two attendants in white uniforms knocked on the door. One was young, appearing to be scrubbed and eager to save the world. The other was probably about fifty; he just looked bored and tired.

"You called for an ambulance?" the older one said.

"Yes I did. I wondered if you got lost."

"No, ma'am, we had three car wrecks. Sorry," the younger one said, having the decency to look embarrassed.

"Where is she?" the older one asked, looking around like I might have propped her up in the hallway.

"She's in her bed. Come this way." As I led the way, I felt a fountain of tears building up. It struck me for the first time that she was gone forever. No more milk and calamine lotion baths, no martinis with five limes. No more tears at night. No more fear of the dark. She was in her own darkness forever now. I fought off the tears.

"Is this how you found her?" the older attendant asked.

"Yes."

"You didn't move anything or change anything?"

"No."

"Well, we have to wait for the police before we can move her."

I nodded. "I sure hope they don't take as long as you did."

"Yes, ma'am," he said, still looking bored. I could see in his eyes the moment he recognized her. He wasn't bored anymore.

"Is that who I think it is?" he asked.

Well, now, I suppose that will depend on who you think she is, now won't it?"

I was surprised by the anger in my voice, and he looked surprised, too.

"Oh, I'm sorry. I'm upset and trying to hold it together. Yes, she is who you think she is."

I sat by the window again, in the cheap, creaking rocker. The rain was coming down like a scene on a movie set with some guy on the roof pouring bucket after bucket. Today, I was to replenish her calamine lotion. She wouldn't need it now. My back hurt, my legs were numb, and my brain burned. When the police arrive, they will ask me a thousand questions, over and over. I have no idea what to tell them.

A tall, slender man in his thirties walked through the open bedroom door. He removed his hat as he said, "Detective Lawrence Milburn, ma'am." He hesitated and then introduced Detective John Williams, a short, robust man starting to lose his hair. He had a nice smile, and he held his hand out to shake mine. When I reached to take it, I watched my hand tremble. Then the tears started. The dam burst. I was flooded. I couldn't help myself. I wasn't sure I loved her, but I did respect her.

My tears were a mystery to me. Maybe I was crying because her Joey came to mind. He would be crushed.

"Ma'am, perhaps we can talk in another room while Detective Williams does his job," Detective Milburn said gently. Detective Williams looked awfully young, maybe twenty-five. I wondered if this was his first call.

I moved to the living room and sat in a blue velvet chair. Her Joey bought her the living room set. It was expensive. The cushions nearly swallowed you up when you sat on them. The opposite wall had a full-length mirror. She always looked at herself in that mirror before she left the house. There were many wee hour nights I found her standing in front of this very mirror, completely naked and in what seemed to be a trance. My vision cleared, and I got a good look at myself in that mirror. I look tired, old, maybe in my fifties. I was barely thirty. My dark hair was pulled back in a bun, and my drab, plaid dress hid my tiny figure. The misses never wanted me to dress nice. I obeyed her. I wished I had done something different on this day. I looked haggard, sickly, and pale. My blue eyes were puffy and red from crying. No makeup. I wasn't permitted to wear any makeup. She insisted I wear "old maid" shoes. You know, the kind schoolmarms wore back in the thirties. I hated them at first but got used to them. I wore no hose, and my plaid dress hung almost to my ankles. That's exactly how she insisted I appear.

I remembered once, her Joey – I called him "Mister Joe" – gave me one hundred dollars and told me to buy nicer clothes. There was hell to pay, and I never accepted another gift from any of her callers. She held one hundred dollars out of my pay that month, saying some of her things were missing. I didn't argue with her; I needed my job. I had no education, no special skills. I knew how lucky I was to have the job. Now, I am out of work.

Detective Milburn cleared his throat to get my attention. "Your name?"
"Yes, I'm sorry, I kind of drifted off, didn't I? I am Elizabeth Dexter. Beth for short."
Detective Milburn's voice was gruff and serious, but his eyes were kind.

"Miss Dexter, can you tell me what happened?"

"I'm not sure. Let's see, last night at ten, she bathed." I watched in the mirror as I placed my left hand to my cheek. My right hand stayed in my lap. I sit stiffly, and in the mirror, I appeared to be attentive, but my mind kept going back to Joey. For a minute, I couldn't remember what I was supposed to be talking about. "Where was I? Oh, yes, she always bathes at ten, then her martini by ten-forty-five, and eleven she was settled in her bed, relaxing. She made a few phone calls, and I left her bedside, I guess, around eleven-thirty."

"Was she excited about anything? You know, agitated? Did she have any company?"

"Why yes, she did. I almost forgot about that. At almost midnight, there was a knock on the door. I had to get up to let him in."

"Who was it, Miss Dexter?"

I sat back in my chair. I wondered if that evil man had anything to do with her death. He was always so hateful and condescending to me. "Peter Wilson, sir. His name is Peter Wilson."

"Peter Wilson, the famous actor?"

"Yes, sir, that's him."

"I see. Did you show him to the bedroom?"

"Oh no, sir. He marched himself right in there like he was angry about something."

"Angry?"

"Yes sir, he definitely had something on his mind. He totally ignored me once the door was opened."

"Did you follow him in?" the detective asked.
"Oh no sir. I tried to stay out of his way."

"Why is that, Miss Dexter?"

"Well, he didn't like me, and I guess you could say the feeling was mutual. I avoided him."

"Did he ever hurt you or say something to hurt you?"

I felt my face flush as I remembered our encounters. "Only every time he came over, except last night. Last night he didn't have any nasty comments about the way I dressed, or the way my hair was fixed. He laughed at my shoes." I lifted them from the floor and looked at them. They really weren't too bad, once you got used to them. I looked up and caught Detective Milburn staring at my shoes. I dropped them back to the floor and saw my feet meeting the floor in the mirror.

"Did you hear any arguing or any banging around or anything?"

"No, I turned off the lights and went back to bed."

"So you don't know when he left."

"No."

"Now, Miss Dexter, can you tell me if he was a frequent evening visitor?" he asked, looking a little embarrassed. It wasn't hard to catch his meaning.

"You mean was there anything going on between them?"

"Yes. I'm sorry to have to ask such a question."

"No, I understand. Some things you must know. There was nothing going on between them. If I may be so bold…"

"Please do."

"He was a mouthpiece for two very famous men she, well, she was seeing."

"I see. Can you tell me who these famous men are?"

In the mirror, I noticed my hands were twitching in my lap. I clasped them together so tight the tips of my fingers went white. I knew this was coming of course, and I still had not figured out how to answer. Maybe I should tell him about the privacy statement I had to sign. The more I thought about last night's visitor, the more I believed the three had something to do with her death. And if they would kill a famous movie star, killing a lowly housekeeper would be like thumping an ant off a red and white checkered picnic table. No. I best not answer that question, I decided.

"Detective Milburn, my employer had many famous visitors."

"Yes, but you said this Wilson fella is a mouthpiece. For whom?"

I cleared my throat and thought carefully about what to say next. "Let's just say they are both high up in our government."

"I see. Yes, I heard that. I understand." He paused and abruptly changed the subject. "Miss Dexter, did you like your employer?"

"Yes, I did. What an odd question."

"No, not really. If you have seen as many cases as I have, you would know sometimes the housekeeper or the butler actually did do it," he said with a slight smile.

"She was a strange duck, no doubt. But, no, I got along with her. I can't say that I liked her every minute and certainly didn't always like what she did, but overall we did okay together. I was number seven in a month's time."

"What?"

"Seven. She went through six housekeepers in one month, before I went to work for her.

"And how did you survive when six others didn't?"

I decided to be frank. "It was easy. I just ignored her."

The detective looked perplexed. "You can't work for someone and ignore them."

"No, that's not what I mean. I ignored her strange ways. If she wanted something her way, I figured she was paying me, so I did it her way. I can see where some would run out of here screaming.
"

"Was she difficult?"

I let out a short laugh before I could stop myself. "Yes, and often."

"I see. Let's get back to her caller last night."

"Okay, but there isn't much I can tell you other than his name. I think you can ask him questions and get better answers."

"Yes, ma'am, we intend to question him. Is there anything else you can tell me? Did you get up during the night and check on her?"

"No, sir. That was a specific order from her. Once she goes to bed, I should never go into her bedroom unless it's after eight-thirty in the morning. Two soft boiled eggs and three slices of dry toast."

"Ma'am?"

"Her breakfast. She would sit up, eat her breakfast, and go back to sleep, but she always wanted it at precisely eight-thirty every morning.

He nodded. "So that's when you found her?"

"Yes."

"But it's nine-thirty now. Did you wait to call the ambulance and police?"

"No, I called at eight thirty-two this morning, after I dropped her breakfast on her bedroom floor. I knew she was dead by just looking at her."

"I see. Did you move or change anything in the bedroom?"

"No. I sat in the rocker in her room, watched it rain, and cried after I called you."

"And you didn't hear any noises after Mr. Wilson arrived?"

"No."

"Well, I see the body…" He hesitated, looking for a way to tell me gently they have taken her away. “I mean the bedroom is clear if you want to clean up the mess on the floor.”

“I will, thank you.”

“Miss Dexter, where can I get in touch with you, if more questions are necessary?”

“Here, I guess. I have no other address. I suppose I will have to wait to see what her lawyers want me to do.”

“Can you tell me her lawyer’s names?”

“Yes, they were here a few months ago, drawing up her will. James Keyes and Bill Ottoman.”

I could tell by his expression the next question would not be pleasant. “Are you in it?”

“I don't know, Detective Milburn. Surely you don’t think...”

"No, Miss Dexter, I don't. I have been on this job for some time. I usually can tell."

"Can tell what?"

"Guilt, Miss Dexter. I can usually smell it."

"Then you need to be sniffing Mr. Wilson." I couldn't believe I had said that. Both hands flew to my mouth to stop it from saying anything else.

"So you will be calling her lawyers and Mister Joe?"

"Mister Joe?"

"He is a good friend. No way could he ever hurt her. I doubt he would know anything about all this."

"And Joe's last name?"

"Please don't ask me that question. I will contact him and he can call you, if that's okay."

"Sure, Miss Dexter. I understand."

As the photographers, the coroner, and the detectives left the house, I stood at the window in her bedroom looking out at the dreary day and watching the ambulance drive away. I realized I would never see my employer again. As odd and strange as she was, she was gone from this earth and it hurt.

I put the receiver back on the telephone (she had apparently dropped it at some point last night) and began looking for her paisley, cloth-covered, personal phone book. It was where I had seen it hundreds of times, tucked behind a cheap plaster lamp. The base of the lamp was much larger than the phone book, so it wasn't in plain sight when the authorities were there.

The phone cord wasn't very long. I sat in the floor with the phone between my legs and my stupid-looking plaid dress hiked up to mid-thigh. I took a moment to compose myself before I thumbed through the book, looking for Mister Joe. He was on the last page, the only name on the page. My hands trembled as I dialed his number. My mind raced desperately looking for the right words to tell him the sad news. I knew it would break his heart.

"Hello."

"Mister Joe?"

"Hello, Beth, how's our girl this morning?" He sounded his always alert and cheerful self.

"Mister Joe." My voice sounded strange to me. I couldn't seem to squeeze the words I had to say around the lump in my throat.

"Yes, Beth, what is it?" he said, starting to sound a little nervous. "Is she all right?"

"No, Mister Joe, she isn't. She was just taken to the morgue."

There was a long pause. "The morgue?" I could tell the word had registered in his brain, but the truth hadn't reached his heart.

"Yes, sir. Can you please come over? I don't know what to do."

"Sure," he said. "I'm on my way. You stay put." There was another pause and he asked once more hoping I suppose, that he had misunderstood. "The morgue?"

"Yes, sir."

CHAPTER TWO

I watched as the powder blue Thunderbird pulled into the driveway. The rocker squeaked, but I hadn't realized I had moved. Her breakfast was still splattered all over the floor. I could see no reason to get in a big hurry cleaning it up. It was almost ten-fifteen in the morning, and the rain was still pouring down. I watched as Mister Joe got out of his car. He did nothing to protect himself from the rain. He was one of the few men I had ever seen who didn't let rain affect them. He walked in the heavy rain as if it were a sun shiny day. I liked him. He was confident. He didn't play silly games. He was exactly what he was. No pretense.

As I opened the door, I fell into his huge, strong arms. He stood in the rain as I clung to him with uncontrollable tears. He froze. He knew now that what I told him was true. I knew he must have prayed hard against what he heard, and he surely had hoped to find her well and smiling. What he found was a sobbing housekeeper.

"Oh, silly me," I said, backing away from him. "I'm sorry. Come on in out of the rain." I ran for a towel. I couldn't look at his eyes. I knew they are full of pain. When I returned from the bathroom with a couple of towels, he was standing like a statue at her bedroom door. He didn't move. Rain dripped from his clothes, and tears dripped from his eyes. His tears came from way down inside him. He was a man's man, one who never cried. For him to allow such a show of emotion, his pain must have been overwhelming.

I bumped his right shoulder and handed him a towel. He took the large bath towel and hung it over his head, his face hidden from me. I put my small hand on his waist and led him into the kitchen. He sat dumbfounded in the vinyl dinette chair as I pulled his wet shoes and socks off. He sat there, motionless.

I used a second towel to dry his feet after removing his shoes and socks. He was like a very old man who couldn't do anything for himself. I stepped behind him and pulled off his jacket. It was soaked through. I took off his shirt, and even his T-shirt was drenched. I pulled the towel away from his face and began to dry his hair. His muscles glistened with raindrops. He was as handsome a man as I had ever seen. He was strong and big, about six feet one and a hundred ninety pounds. I recalled reading that on one of his baseball cards. He gave it to me when I was a housekeeper for him and the misses, when they were married. I treasured his gift and often used it as a bookmarker. The misses never knew he gave me his baseball card.

I stripped him down to his pants, gave him two more towels, and left him sitting at the table. When I came back ten minutes later, he had not moved a muscle.

"Mister Joe, you need to remove these wet clothes, sir. I have some clothes the misses kept saying she was going to give you. I guess its stuff you left from before."
He didn't move. I've never seen him so still.

"Mister Joe." I took his face into my hands and made him look up at me. "Mister Joe, you need to dress in dry clothes; you will catch your death."

I regretted saying that instantly: "death." It just fell out of my mouth. I wasn't doing a very good job of controlling my thoughts or words.

He stood and unbuckled his belt. I left the room.

I cleaned up the spilled breakfast and scrubbed the carpet to remove the stain from the small glass of orange juice. As I scrubbed the carpet with a damp cloth, I felt him enter the room. I looked up and he was standing in the doorway, his massive, strong hand clenching the doorframe.

"Mister Joe, you wait for me in the kitchen, please."
He walked over to the bedroom window and watched the rain as it fell even heavier than

before. I watched him from the corner of my eye. He was like a beaten man. I'd never seen him less than on top of the world. He looked a foot shorter. Drawn.

"Mister Joe, please wait for me in the kitchen. I will be right there."
He turned and looked down at me.

"Why did this happen?" His voice broke. "We talked every night. Last night, she was fine. She was all excited about a new movie role."

My heart ached for him. "Mister Joe, listen to me. Go to the kitchen. I put on a fresh pot of coffee, and it should be ready. Please, let me finish up in here."

Mister Joe walked away from the window and gave a deep stare to her bed. He walked past me like I wasn't there. His silence was worse than when I was alone in silence. His bare feet, still wet. No shirt, no T-shirt, just dry trousers. From behind, he looked as though he had just crawled out of bed and he was going for a cup of coffee. His hair all tussled from my scrubbing it earlier with a towel.

He never talked much. The misses hated that. I heard him tell her once, "When I got something to say, I will speak up." At that moment, he had nothing to say. He was moving slow. He left the bedroom, dazed.

As I entered the kitchen, I found him in the same chair, a puddle of rainwater at his feet. I had dried off his feet, but he had stepped in the collected water on the floor.
I set the breakfast tray on the counter next to the sink, mopped up the floor, and dried his feet again, swiping his face with a fresh new towel. It wasn't rain I was dabbing off of his face.

"Mister Joe, I need you to snap out of this, sir. I need your help."

Mister Joe slowly turned his head toward me as I finished cleaning up the wet floor. "Of course you do," he said softly.

I had never heard him speak softly before. When he spoke, he spoke with thunder. He didn't shout, but he had a loud, booming voice, full of life and exuberance. Now I could barely hear him.

As many miscarriages as she suffered - three with Mister Joe - concealing a live birth was easy for her. Far too easy. She didn't want him to know she had birthed a girl. The baby was tiny, about nine weeks premature. She made me take her and the baby to the hospital. I figured she was going to get the little girl some help. What she did stunned me. She had her attorneys meet us at the hospital, and she signed that baby over for adoption. That sweet little helpless baby girl, Mister Joe's baby girl, she gave it away.

Her attorneys didn't try to stop her, and the hospital folks didn't ask any questions. No one tried to stop her. I was screaming inside, but I knew my place. I said nothing. I just listened. The baby went to Chasement Adoption Home in Ooltawah, Tennessee. She wanted the child not only out of the state, but as far away as possible. What a sad thing! I watched her over the years, and I think she felt threatened by a baby. I wondered sometimes, if the miscarriages weren't helped along. She and Mister Joe broke up a few months after that, and we came back here to live. She never gave up her home. Mister Joe was devastated.

He had lost his only true love, and he had been deprived of his daughter. Sometimes the misses would go into rages, fits, and other times she seemed so normal, but I knew she wasn't thinking clearly when she gave the baby away. She couldn't have known what she was doing.

The lawyers didn't care; they made money. The hospital didn't care. Only two people knew whom the baby's mother was, and they were sworn to secrecy. The misses' lawyers would have had them for lunch if they told, and they knew it.

Poor Mister Joe. He looked like a broken man, sitting in her kitchen. Feeble. He was reduced to feeble. I had to help him through this, but I couldn't tell him about his daughter. Those lawyers would ruin my life. It hadn't been a bad life. Of course, I had to tolerate a lot from the misses, but there was nothing she did that I couldn't handle. Those attorneys, well, I couldn't take them on, so I had to keep her secret.

"Mister Joe, can I get you a cup of coffee?"

"Yes, please," he said, quietly.

But still, it was a reaction. He was reacting to my voice. That was a positive sign.
I poured two cups of coffee and sat across from him at the table, something I was never permitted to do when the misses was alive.

"Mister Joe, we need to call her attorneys, her agent and publicist."

"What do we tell them?" he whispered.

"Well, we need to let them know she is ... she is no longer with us."

"Yeah," he said, "I suppose you're right." He stood slowly, taking a second to get his legs under him. He walked over to the wall phone.

"Mr. Keyes? This is Joe. She is dead." He said it flatly, trying to keep emotion out of his voice. "Yes, the housekeeper found her this morning." There was a pause while the person on the other end of the line took in the news, and then Mister Joe said, "Yes, that's right. Okay, I will."

Mister Joe hung up. He stood there a moment and then called her agent.

This time his voice shook as he broke the news. "Stephen? Yes, this is Joe. She is gone buddy. She died last night. Okay, yes, I will be here, at her home. Okay. Goodbye."

He made one more call, to a man named Oliver, and then he turned to me at the kitchen table.

"They are all on their way over here, Beth. I suggest you collect yourself. They will have tons of questions for you."

"Mister Joe, is it all right if I clean up and change my clothes?" I wasn't sure why, but I felt so uneasy in those clothes. I just wanted to get them off.

"Of course, Beth. And, Beth, I know she made you wear those drab clothes. You can wear whatever you like now."

"Thank you, Mister Joe, but I think I will wear whatever the misses wanted. I don't want to show no disrespect."

He smiled at me and said, "As you wish."

I left him sipping a hot cup of coffee. I cringed as I walked past her bedroom. There was an odd feeling deep in my stomach. I quickly showered and dressed. As I stood in front of the mirror, I didn't look any different than I did before. I didn't mind. The last thing I wanted to do right now was doll up. Those damned attorneys would have me up on first-degree murder charges if I gave them the slightest provocation.

Twenty minutes later, I was back in the kitchen. It was nearly noon, and I knew I didn't have time to prepare a meal, so I began slicing tomatoes and tearing lettuce for a help-yourself tray of turkey and ham sandwiches.

Mister Joe was still making calls. He had pulled a dinette chair under the wall phone and had fished his small phone book from his wallet. He was organized like that. Everything had a place. When they were together, I quickly learned that he was a perfectionist. He seemed to always be prepared. The initial shock of her death was wearing off, though his face was still lined with sorrow, but he was back in charge.

I had an intense desire to tell him he had a four-year-old daughter, in hopes of softening his pain. I knew it would give him great pleasure to realize that a part of the woman he had loved was still alive.

I opened my mouth, thinking how to phrase the news, but a knock at the door interrupted me, and I took it as a sign to keep my mouth shut. It was those damned attorneys, Keyes and Ottoman. James Keyes was a mousy-looking man, with thin, light hair and large, blue, piercing eyes. He always dressed in an expensive business suit. He looked as though he used to be an athlete, but now he was getting a little pudgy around the middle.

Bill Ottoman, his partner, was exactly the opposite. He was a perfectionist in the way he dressed and in his grooming. His flashing brown eyes said "friend," but his reputation said otherwise. He was trim, had a full head of brown hair, and he had a healthy glow that made it seem he had just come from the gym. I had heard Ottoman and Mister Joe talk about running. Ottoman told Mister Joe he ran five miles a day, no matter the weather. The weather today would have been a problem, with twenty-five mile-an-hour winds and heavy rain.

I opened the door and showed the two men into the kitchen. Their briefcases were bulging. The fine leather, wet from the rain. I gave them bath towels to dry off.

"Morning, Joe," Keyes said. Ottoman gave Mister Joe a bear hug as Mister Joe stood.

"I am sorry you lost a very good friend. We can't imagine what happened to her,"

Ottoman said with such feeling, I had to wonder if any attorney could be that sincere.

"We don't know what happened to her, Bill. Beth here called me this morning and told me she had been taken to the morgue."

"Okay, first things first. We want a sealed coroner's report," Keyes snapped.

"Why would we want that?" Mister Joe asked.

"Well, in case she, umm, did herself in."

Mister Joe looked ready to poke Keyes in the mouth.

"She would never do that," he said, raising his voice for the first time since he walked in the door that morning.

"Now, Joe," Ottoman said, "you just said you don't know the cause of death. Allow us protect her and her memory."

Mister Joe sighed. "Okay, but I can tell you now her funeral will not be a circus. You hear me? A closed casket, and close friends only. I mean it."

"Joe, we understand your wishes. I read her will on the way over here, and that doesn't conflict with any last instructions she left. I will set it up just as you wish."

"Good," Mister Joe barked. His eyes were aflame as he stared at Keyes. That attorney had Mister Joe all riled up.

"Now, let's focus. My best guess is the funeral will be in three days. Is there anything in particular you want said or done?"

"Yes," Mister Joe said without hesitation. "I want perpetual flowers on her grave. Fresh cut flowers every day."

"Okay, Joe, what sort of flowers?"

"She loved long-stemmed red roses."

"Done," Ottoman said. "What else?" He was doing all the talking now. Keyes knew he had hit a sore spot, and I think he decided to keep quiet.

"Well, I want to be front row in the chapel. I want Beth here by my side. She will need a vault at a mausoleum. I want the one next to her, so when you buy, buy two."

"Okay, Joe," Ottoman said, but I could tell there was a problem.

"Joe, now be calm until I explain this to you, okay? Give me a chance to say what I have to say, then we can discuss it, and you decide what you want to do." Ottoman hesitated, choosing his words carefully.

"Okay," Mister Joe said, "but don't you start with this suicide stuff; I know better."

"Of course not," Ottoman said hastily. "James meant no harm, Joe. He was looking ahead, trying to protect her, that's all."

"Okay, I suppose you are right, both of you. But let's not bring that up again."

"Okay, Joe, whatever you say. Now look, I can do everything you asked except one thing."

"What?" Mister Joe asked. I could see the fire flash back into his eyes.

"Joe, it's not proper to have a housekeeper on the front row. People will talk."

"So let them talk," he said, dismissing Ottoman's concern with a wave of his hand.

"Only close friends will be there anyway. No damn reporters. Just close friends. No one else." He glared into Ottoman's eyes. "I mean that!"

"Okay, Joe, we will invite close friends only, but there is this matter in her will that may change your mind." Ottoman glanced at me uneasily and cleared his throat.

"She left the housekeeper a large sum of money, Joe."

My heart jumped. Why on earth would she leave me anything? I wondered what a "large sum" meant. I was good to her, I obeyed her wishes, but I didn't think that was enough to make her want to leave me money, especially a lot of money.

"Well, if she left Beth money, then she wanted Beth to have it. That's not so difficult to understand."

"No, Joe, and we will respect her wishes, but to have the housekeeper at your side at her funeral, and take into account a lot of money and her mysterious death, I just think we are asking for trouble, Joe. That's all. Now, I will do whatever you wish, but at least think this through before you decide."

Mister Joe didn't hesitate. "I have thought it through. Beth sits with me. Period."

She left a lot of money? I felt faint. My legs wobbled; my head was spinning. I felt butterflies in my stomach. Mister Joe's face blurred and grew dim. The room went dark. I collapsed on the floor.

CHAPTER THREE

I came around slowly. At first, I couldn't remember what had happened, then I knew: My legs just buckled. Mister Joe had caught my head before it hit the hard tiled kitchen floor. He was cradling me in his arms.

"You're okay, Beth. You just fainted." Mister Joe's reassuring voice helped me find my way back to reality.
I stood, wobbling a bit, and Mister Joe helped me to a chair. There I sat with people I wasn't permitted to sit with the day before. A lot of money changes some folks' way of thinking, I told myself.

"Now, Beth, are you okay?" Ottoman asked.

"Yes sir, I think so."

Ottoman leaned toward me as he spoke. His had eaten eggs with garlic for breakfast. I could smell both.

“Beth, can you tell us what happened last night?” Ottoman continued.

“Nothing out of the ordinary, except at eleven-thirty last night, Peter Wilson was banging on the front door. I let him in, and he stormed into the misses’ room. I went back to bed. I don’t know when he left.”

A look of concern crossed Ottoman’s face. “Peter Wilson? Hmm … did you tell the police this?”

“Of course.”

“I see.” Ottoman leaned back into his chair and gazed at Keyes.

“That was my first thought too, Bill,” Keyes said matter-of-factly. “Those guys had her done in.”

Mister Joe leaped from his seat, reached Keyes in two steps, and grabbed him by the collar. With one motion, Mister Joe had Keyes against the wall. I don’t ever remember seeing a man’s eyes bulge with terror like that but Keyes was seeing his life pass before him, no doubt.

Ottoman stood and tried to break Mister Joe's grip, but he was wasting his time. Mister Joe had a grip so tight, a twenty ton truck could not have separated anger and enemy. Keyes's expensive suit started to rip.

"Joe, let go of him!" Ottoman hollered.

Mister Joe's eyes had been pink from his tears, but now they were red and alive with anger. He wanted to strike back. His love of his life was dead, and he was ready to send someone else along to a forever sleep. Keyes seemed to be that person at the moment.

I placed a soft and gentle hand on his left forearm. "Mister Joe, you are attacking the wrong person," I said. "I have to agree with Mister Keyes, though I certainly don't like his manner. I do think Peter Wilson may have had something to do with her death."

I could feel Mister Joe's grip loosen. God, that man was strong as a bull! I supposed he had to be to have slammed so many home runs. He had taught me what RBI meant – runners batted in. I read an article once that had the whole world excited. Mister Joe had hit a ball and made it to a base in fifty-something games in a row. It's called a hitting streak, or something. Now I knew how he did it. He was very strong. Mister Joe wasn't a regular kind of guy. If he ever got his hands on Peter Wilson, it would be goodbye from this world. It wouldn't be a big loss, for me, anyway, that mister uppity.

As Mister Joe's grip loosened, he dumped Keyes back into his chair in a heap.

"Tell me what I need to know about her death!" Mister Joe demanded as he fixed his eyes on Keyes's nose. I could almost hear it breaking.

Ottoman backed up a few steps before he spoke. "Now Joe, we didn't want to be the ones to tell you this, but she has been seeing brothers in high government positions."

"Who are they?"

"Now, Joe, calm down. We don't know for sure, but we talked about it on the way over here this morning. We can only guess that she knew too much. You know, they told her stuff she shouldn't know. We think maybe ... now, just maybe ... they silenced her."

Mister Joe quieted down. He had heard rumors, she had mentioned the brothers a few times, but this scenario had never occurred to Mister Joe. As he sat back down, everyone in the room could hear his heavy breathing. It scared me. I could visualize him snapping a man in two with no effort.

"Tell you what," Ottoman said. "I'm going to send James down to the coroner's office and let him see if he can find out anything. Okay?"

"Sure." Mister Joe answered, still breathing hard.

Ottoman motioned Keyes toward the front door. He left quickly, relieved to get out of there.

It was the last time I ever saw Keyes.

Ottoman stood and looked over at the counter.

"Beth, did you do this for us?" I nodded, and Ottoman started to make himself a sandwich. He encouraged Mister Joe to do the same. We both sat at the table, both enveloped in our memories, occasionally I would look over at Mister Joe. He had gone from an old man stupor to a really strong, pissed off guy. He stared at the floor, seething at whatever thoughts he was having.

Someone knocked at the front door. Stephen, her agent, was soaked, and all the water on his face wasn't rain. He truly loved the misses. He and Mister Joe sat on the back, covered patio for more than an hour. Ottoman, finally left without saying goodbye. I thought maybe it was good for Mister Joe to talk with another man who loved her. But when I went outside to see if they wanted anything, they weren't talking. They were just sitting, each probably lost in their own memories of her.

The next ten days passed in a blur. When it was over, I couldn't remember the funeral. Mister Joe stayed in her house with me for those ten days. He kept mostly to himself. A few ballplayers came over for a brief visit, a time, or two. Mister Joe wasn't much company. He usually just sat there staring at the floor.

The attorneys told me I had to move. Mister Joe tried to intervene, but to no avail. They had already sold her home at an unbelievable, astronomical price. The will was to be read that afternoon. Mister Joe told me he would drive me to the attorney's office. It was the first time I had ever ridden in his car. It was a nice car, very nice. The plush leather seats make me feel like I had money. That was about to come true, of course, if the lawyers hadn't figured out a way to cheat me out of it.

As Mister Joe's blue Thunderbird pulled up to Brook Hills Professional Building just outside Los Angeles, it was ten forty-five in the morning. Mister Joe found a parking spot and quickly got out to open my door. That made me smile. I felt cleansed and squeaky clean from the rush of fresh air, riding in his convertible. He took a few steps ahead so he could open the building door for me as well. The elevator was an express to the sixteenth floor. We sat in an impressive outside lounge and declined a secretary's offer of coffee or cola. Mister Joe seemed nervous, maybe anxious. I suppose he could have been angry. As I said earlier, he didn't talk much.

A young lady in her twenties asked us to follow her. We entered a huge office with a beautiful, long, wooden conference table. Bill Ottoman sat alone, engrossed in his paperwork. Mister Joe cleared his throat.

"Oh, hey, guys, come on in and have a seat," Ottoman said. I wanted to sit at the opposite end of the table, but Mister Joe pointed to a seat near Ottoman. "Joe, Miss Dexter, let me sum this up for you," he said.

"No, Bill, we prefer to hear the will as she intended it. " Joe said. "Neither of us wants an abbreviated version. Just read the document, Bill."

"I'm sorry, but I simply can't do that."

"And why… simply, not?" Joe demanded.

"Well, because some of it is personal regarding the both of you. I don't think it would be a good idea for both of you to be present at the same time."

I watched these two men try to stare each other down. Maybe there was a reason she left me a wad of money. No telling what I would have to do for it. I knew all along there had to be a catch! My misses did everything for a purpose. Sometimes that purpose was lost to me, but I knew her well enough to know that everything she did was always thought out, in advance.

"Mister Joe, I don't mind waiting outside. You take care of your business. Mr. Ottoman, call me when you are ready for me."

I knew a lot of money was too good to be true! But, I wondered, what on earth could she want me to do? I settled back into the same lounge and waited. This time the young lady didn't ask. She politely set a cold cola with a straw near my seat. She smiled and said, "Enjoy."

I had never had a Coke with a straw before, and I wasn't starting now. Straw in hand, I just turned it up. I looked around and didn't see anyone watching as I tossed the straw in the wastebasket. I sat there for no more than twenty minutes. Mister Joe came into the small lounge and said, "Beth, it's your turn. If there is anything you don't understand, or if you just want my help, I will be right here."

"Thank you, Mister Joe," I told him, and I started that long walk down the corridor that seemed to have no end. I eased my way back into the conference room. The largest barn I've ever seen wasn't as big as his office.

"Come in, Miss Dexter. Have a seat near me, if you like." I took a chair four down from him. I wondered if he smelled like eggs and garlic again.

"Now, Ms. Dexter, it seems your employer wanted to leave you a sizable amount of money."

"How much?" I asked as my throat went dry.

"Five hundred thousand dollars."

It took me a minute to catch my breath. "That's a lot of money, Mister Ottoman."

"Yes, my dear, it is. I was thinking, we have an investment group here in our offices, and, if you like, we can invest it for you and help you make more."

"Well, that's mighty nice of you, sir, but the amount is plenty. I prefer it in cash."

Ottoman chuckled. "Well," he said, "it doesn't happen quite like that, Miss Dexter."
"Just how does it happen, Mister Ottoman?"

"We will write you a check from your employer's account."

"I see. Then I can take it to a bank and get cash?"

Ottoman tried to smile, but it looked more like a grimace. "Yes, you can, but I'm not so sure that is a smart thing to do."

"Mister Ottoman, I'm not a smart person. I will take a check, please."

"I see," he said. He was beginning to realize there was no way of talking me into leaving that money in his hands. There was no doubt in my mind he wanted my money, and I was determined to leave that office with a check.

"Well, my dear, there are some stipulations."

I wasn't surprised. I had been expecting a bomb, and now here it comes. The other shoe is about to fall.

"What sort of stipulations?"

"You will recall that, four years ago, your employer gave birth."

"Yes."

"She placed that baby girl up for adoption."

"Yes, we were both there - you and me, I mean."

"Your employer wants you to follow that child's life. She doesn't say anything in here about intervening or anything. She just wants someone to watch over the child."

"I'm not sure what that means, Mister Ottoman."

He shrugged. "I asked her when she gave me that stipulation. She never answered."

"I see."

"The most important thing is that you never tell Mister Joe. She was determined that he not find out about the baby."

"I can do that, but I am not sure exactly what else I am supposed to do."

He stared at the paper, as if he couldn't quite believe what he was seeing. "She says here just that you are to watch over the child. I will leave that to your discretion. But I must tell you that if Mister Joe ever finds out, you will forfeit the money."

"I understand. How do I find this child?"

"She was placed at Chasement Adoption Home, Ooltawah, Tennessee."

"Yes, but Mister Ottoman, how do I find her? I mean, you gave me the adoption agency, but what if she was adopted."

He was getting bored, I could see, and I figured it wouldn't be long before he turned the topic back to his real interest: my newly acquired money.

"That will have to be your decision, Miss Dexter. Frankly, I have no idea what your employer expected of you, other than to keep her secret."

"I see. Well, okay. Thank you. Is my check ready?"

At the mention of money, he smiled broadly again and leaned toward me. "Now, are you sure you want that much money? Perhaps we can invest half of it for you."

"No, sir, I prefer my check now, please."

Minutes later, I had the check in my hand and I was heading back to the lounge. If he hadn't written for it me, I would have gone to get Mister Joe. Keyes and Ottoman saw firsthand what happened when Mister Joe got mad. Ottoman didn't want to mix with Mister Joe. I felt strong and confident knowing Mister Joe was down the hall. As I approached the lounge, Mister Joe stood.

"You okay?"

"Yes sir, thank you. I'm fine. She left me a lot of money."

"Yes, Beth, I know. We both lived with her, and I know you earned every dime. Now tell me, where would you like to go?"

I was astonished as it hit me: I hadn't thought one minute past getting this check in my hand. "I don't know. The last nine years have been so wrapped up in the misses, I haven't given any thought to what I might do next. I know I have to be out of the house by five this afternoon. I guess I have nowhere to go, Mister Joe."

He laughed, and I wondered if he was making fun of me in some way.

"Sweet Beth, you have a lot of money now. I'll take charge. Do you mind?"
"No, sir. I have no idea what to do."

"First stop, Beth, is the bank. Let's get you some cash."

I nodded enthusiastically. "Cash is good, Mister Joe."

He laughed again and took my arm. "You bet it is!"

In about twenty minutes, we pulled into a bank parking lot. He stopped the car and turned it off. He sat there.

I could feel my hands trembling and my face getting red.

"Mister Joe, will you go in with me? I've never been inside a bank."
He turned to stare at me.

"What?"

"No, sir. The misses gave me enough cash to get by on, and I sent my mama a little. I never had any left over. I had no need to go to a bank."

"Beth," he said, smiling broadly, "you never cease to amaze me. You are a real throwback to forty years ago. Let's open you up a savings account so it will draw interest and open you a checking account with, say, ten grand."

I nodded, and Mister Joe explained how it all worked. I was grateful he was there to help me through this. At my insistence, Mister Joe was placed on both of my new accounts. I'm not sure why I insisted on that but I trusted him.

Once I was all done, we decided not to return to the misses' house. Mister Joe said I wouldn't need those drab clothes anymore, so I would lose nothing by leaving them where they were. I never intended to wear anything drab again.

Mister Joe showed me how cashier's checks worked. I told him I wanted to visit relatives in Ooltawah, and he explained about flying and how to get a ticket. He laughed when I told him I had no idea where Ooltawah was.

"I don't know where it is, either," he said.

We stopped at a fancy clothing store. I was very uncomfortable. The women looked at me funny and the prices were way more than I felt right about spending. Mister Joe took me to a small dress shop. The owner was a sweet woman in her late fifties. Mister Joe told her I needed an ensemble. That's what I got, as far as I could tell. When we left the store, I had new clothes for ten days. Mister Joe drove me to a nice, mid-priced hotel. He knew fancy made me uneasy. He checked me in and told me he would be back at eight the next morning. I was to be ready to travel.

As I entered my hotel room, I was surprised by how nice it was. If this wasn't a fancy hotel, I couldn't imagine what a fancy room would look like. I was happy, scared, and alone. I didn't touch anything in that room. I was afraid I might break something. I sat at the

window and looked at the beautiful skyline. My room was twelve stories up. I was in deep thought about the baby girl I had to find when a knock on the door startled me. I nearly jumped out of my seat. Why on earth would anyone be knocking at my door?
I cracked the door a bit and saw a bellhop. He had on one of those silly round caps with a chinstrap.

"Miss Dexter?"

"Yes?"

"A gentleman just delivered this to the front desk. He asked that we bring it up to you."

"What is it?" I couldn't see through the small crack I allowed in the door.

"Ma'am, if you will permit me to enter, I will show you."

"Okay." I stepped back from the door as the bellhop flopped a brown leather suitcase on my bed.

"That is beautiful," I said, not to the bellhop, but to myself, out loud.

"Oh, yeah, he said for me to tell you not to worry about my tip. He gave it to me in advance."

With that, the bellhop slammed the door behind him. I lifted up the case to see the handle. In gold were two single letters; B.D. Mister Joe had my initials put on the suitcase! What a perfect gift. I hadn't thought of needing one, but Mister Joe thought of everything.

The next morning at seven-thirty, I was downstairs waiting for Mister Joe. The desk clerk kept looking at me. I wondered if I owed him any money. I placed my suitcase next to a chair and walked over to him. I could hear my new clothes swish as I walked. It is a new sound to me.

"Excuse me, I was in room twelve-thirteen last night. Can you tell me if I owe anything?"

"Miss Dexter, you paid in advance when you checked in yesterday. Your bill is satisfied, thank you. I hope your stay was a good one."

"Yes. Yes, it was. Thank you. I saw you looking at me and I thought maybe I owed your hotel something."

"No, ma'am. I'm sorry if I was staring." He blushed a little and wouldn't meet my eyes.

"You just look so pretty this morning."

"What?" I couldn't quite believe what I was hearing.

"You look very pretty this morning, ma'am."

I blushed. "Thank you," I said as I turned away. Now, that's a first, I thought. No one had ever told me that before. Of course, the last nine years, I looked like a schoolmarm that you would see in a silent movie.

I lit up when I saw Mister Joe come in the front door. I smiled, as he got closer. He picked up my suitcase and smiled back.

"Did you have a good night?" he asked.

"Yes, it was quite exciting. Thank you for the suitcase."
"Exciting?"

"Well, you know different."

"I see." He smiled an understanding smile. "My pleasure on the suitcase, Beth. I'm glad you like it. Well, let's get to the airport."

"Yes, I guess it's time. It might sound silly, but I'm afraid to fly."

"Not silly at all. Most people are afraid to fly. If God wanted us to fly, he would have given us wings," Mister Joe said as he laughed. He was certainly in a good mood, laughing and talking. He tossed my suitcase in the trunk and opened the car door for me. As he settled into his seat, he looked over at me and said, "You really are a pretty woman."

"Thank you." I could feel the blush return. "The desk man told me that just before you came in."

"The desk man?" Mister Joe laughed louder than I had ever heard him laugh before.

"Beth, I want you to relax and enjoy your airplane ride. I hope your visit goes well. Any thoughts about what you will do after your visit?"

"No."

"Well, if you need my help, look inside the silk lining of your suitcase. I put my phone number there for you. For emergencies, you know."

"That was very thoughtful, Mister Joe. Thank you."

The airport wasn't busy. Mister Joe spoke with the counter man and found out Ooltawah was just outside Chattanooga. One transfer in Atlanta and I should be in Chattanooga by six. Mister Joe told me to ask for a cab to Ooltawah. He walked me to my gate and stayed until passengers began boarding the plane. Mister Joe took me by total surprise and hugged me goodbye. I didn't want to let go. It was the first time I had been so close that I could feel his breath and heartbeat. I didn't want that hug to end. I lingered until I knew I had to let him go. I stepped back, head down. He smiled and turned me towards the aircraft.

I sat on the plane, trying desperately to see Mister Joe though the small, round window. The airplane begin moving away from where we boarded and traveling so fast I lost sight of the terminal. The plane's motion stopped and there was a deafening noise. I closed my eyes as my stomach did a few flips. A few minutes later, it was almost like sitting in that cheap rocker of the misses'. Some creaks and groans, but comfortable nonetheless as we left Mother Earth and reached where the bids fly. The airplane propellers were spinning so fast they appeared to not be moving at all. Maybe the excitement had worn me out because, before I knew it, I was sound asleep. The next thing I knew, I felt like I was on a bucking bronco as the plane landed in Atlanta, a bounce and a bump. A nice lady in a gray uniform showed me where to wait for the flight to Chattanooga. Fifty-five minutes later, I was in the air again. I got brave and ventured a quick glimpse out the window. Everything look so small and getting smaller. Chattanooga was a thirty-minute flight from Atlanta. We didn't get up good before I felt us going back down.

As the plane rolled to a stop, it occurred to me: I had no idea how to find that baby my misses had given up four years ago.

CHAPTER FOUR

As I walked out of the Chattanooga terminal, the heat and humidity took my breath away. I felt a little lightheaded, and it only got worse when a fast talking man in a wool uniform grabbed my suitcase and tried to take it away from me.

"Stop!" I demanded. "What are you doing?"

"I'm your taxi driver, ma'am. Where to?"

"Oh. Well, I need to go to Ooltawah."

"Yes 'sum. I can do that for you. It's about fifteen minutes from here. Know the address?"

"I need a hotel."

"Yes 'sum. That would be Eight Days Inn. It's the only hotel they got there."

"Is it nice?"

He scratched his chin and considered the question. “Well, I suppose some might think it’s nice enough, but I’ve seen much better. My name is Jake. Most folks round about call me J.”

“Okay, Jake, Eight Days Inn, it is.”

His taxi smelled a little funny to me. I couldn’t quite tell what the odor was, but something smelled a little off. As I settled into the back seat, he started talking again.

“Who you visiting?” he asked.

“Distant relatives.”

“What’s their name?”

“Oh, well, you wouldn’t know them.”

Yes ‘sum, I most probably would know ’em. I growed up there.”

I didn’t really want to talk to this man. He talked with a funny twang that made him hard to understand. And I had a lot on my mind.

“Sir, if you don’t mind, I’m really tired and prefer to not talk.”

“Yes ‘sum, that's fine. You can just listen. See that there water tower?”

“Yes, I can see it.” I signed heavily, hoping he would take the hint, but Jake didn’t seem to notice.

“Well, me and my brother used to climb it and think we owned all we could see. Yes sir that was when we were just boys.” His smile faded. “He got in a brawl at the Dew Drop Inn last year. Man cut him up bad. He didn’t make it.”

“Oh, I’m sorry!” I could think of anything else to say.

“It’s no big deal. He was pretty miserable anyhow. Yes ‘sum, when we topped that water tower, we owned all we could see. Some nights we'd just sit up there and rule our kingdom. Our daddy was a drunk. Going home, we got a beating, so some nights we just stayed put up yonder on that there water tower."

After a few minutes of silence, I asked, "How much farther, driver?"

"Jake, ma'am, the name is Jake. We have 'bout five minutes to go. Say, you come from a big town or something? Mighty fine luggage you have there. Yes sir, you can always tell folks with money by their luggage."

I sat back and took in the rolling hills and the Cumberland Mountains beyond. They were beautiful. It seemed quiet here, slow and easy going. I didn't see anyone in a hurry. Not like Hollywood, where everyone moved as if they are late for something.
The taxi pulled up to a bright pink, one-story stucco hotel.

"Well ma'am, here you be, all safe and sound."

"How much do I owe you?"

"Three dollars, ma'am."

"Here's a five; keep the change," I said, thinking that Mister Joe would do the same. I missed having Mister Joe around. He was so strong. He knew so much about everything.

Jake bounced out of the driver's seat and flung my door open. "You go right on in, ma'am," he said. "I will get your luggage."

"Thank you."

The oppressive heat slapped me in the face as the door opened. Seven steps and I was inside a tiny office. A plump woman in her mid-forties wearing pink curlers in her hair was sitting behind a glass enclosure. There was a circle cut in the glass that you were supposed to be able to talk to her through. It would have been about shoulder high for Mister Joe. I had to lean up to the glass stretching up on my toes.

"Excuse me. I need a room, please."

She didn't get up. She sat there reading her afternoon paper. Without looking up, she asked me, "How long you staying?"

That was something I hadn't really thought about.

"Three nights, please," I told her.
"That will be thirty dollars and twelve cents," she said. She remained fixed on her newspaper. I opened my purse and pulled out two twenties. As I set them on the counter, I noticed another small hole in the glass enclosure, half-moon shaped. I hadn't seen this woman move, but my change lay in waiting for me to pick it up.

"Hey, Mabel," Jake said heartily as he lugged my suitcase inside. "Henry around?"

"No, Jake, Henry is at the diner." Mabel held her paper in front of her and talked through it.

The diner. I realized I was hungry.

"Jake, is the diner far from here?" I asked.

"No ma'am, nothing is far from here, unless you leave town," he said, and then giggled at his own joke. "Give me your key and I will drop off your bag and show you the diner. You hungry? Don't eat the stew. It's always two days old. Order you a sandwich. Nobody eats the stew."

I handed Jake my key, he disappeared out the door, and he was back in seconds.

"Your room is third door down, room six. I put your suitcase on your bed for you. Now let's get you something to eat."

This total stranger was taking control of me, and it made me a little uneasy. I had never seen him before and already he was telling me what to do.

"Thank you," I said, "But if you will just point the way..."

"Oh, shoot, I'm hungry, too."

It was obvious I wasn't going to get rid of him, so I followed his fast stride across the street and just a few feet north of the hotel. I paid attention so I would know how to get back. I had no idea the diner was just across the street.

"Hello, everybody!" Jake bellowed as we walked in. Nobody paid him any attention. They all stared at me.

Jake called Ethel, the waitress, over to us as we stood in the doorway.

"Ethel, now you take good care of my new friend here. She is tired and hungry. Don't you go pawning off that sorry stew on her, now, you hear?"

I smiled at Ethel. She was thin and, judging from the way she held herself, she was tired. She looked like she was in her late thirties, but when someone was as tired as this woman appeared to be it was hard to tell. She might have been a pretty woman a few years ago. She had a nice smile, but she wore way too much lipstick and eye shadow. I followed her to a booth. As I sat, I hoped Jake would find someone else to sit with. He did.

"What will you have, ma'am?" Ethel's Southern accent fell hard on my ears. She had a nasal twang and a high-pitched, loud voice that actually hurt my ears.

I looked over at Jake and smiled. "I think I want a sandwich, ham and cheese, please."

"Fries?" she asked.

My eyes darted toward Jake. He shook his head violently.

"No, no fries, thank you. A Coke to drink, please."

Ethel took the small menu from me and left. There were six customers scattered around the diner. My novelty must have worn off quickly because they had gone back to talking to each other and eating their food. I was relieved.

I looked out the plate-glass window. I could see the hotel at an angle from where I sat. The town looked small, dirty and backwards. There wasn't much traffic on what I thought must be the main street. The diner was small and old, with a cracked tile floor. There were nine stools at the bar, where Jake sat, and four booths.

Ethel came back to my table with a glass of ice water. She gave me a weary smile as she placed the glass on the table. It slid a couple of inches from the moisture on the bottom of the glass. Ethel paid no attention. The water looked pale brown. Not like Hollywood's crystal clear water. As I brought it up to my mouth, I detected a faint odor. It taste okay, but it sure smelled and looked funny.

"Oh, honey, don't let the smell or color fool you," Ethel said. "It's perfectly good water. All our water around here smells and looks funny to newcomers. What's your business in Ooltawah?"

The customers all turned to listen to my answer.

"I'm just passing through," I lied.

"Honey, no one just passes through Ooltawah. You either coming here or you not." She chuckled as she placed my plate on the table. My plate had fries. I could see why Jake had tried to warn me. They had grease oozing out of them, and they looked like they had been fried in old grease. I began eating my ham sandwich as Ethel returned to my table.

"I told that old fool in the kitchen you didn't want fries," she said.

"Oh, it's okay. I just don't eat them. Never have."

"Well, you would say that after you have tried Hank's fries. The man can't cook worth a damn. Frieda, that's Hank's wife, is off on

Tuesdays. She does charity work for the orphan's home on Tuesday. Collecting money, blankets and such. Any other day of the week is a good day to eat here, but not today. That's why most folks don't come in on Tuesdays."

"Where is the orphanage?" I asked, trying to act nonchalant.

"About a five-minute walk from here. Just yonder beyond the railroad tracks," she said, pointing out the window. "Eveline Crowley runs it. I hear tell the helper she had ran off 'bout a week ago."

"Really?"

Her smile warmed a bit. "Look, honey," she said as she sat opposite me in the booth, "You don't have a baby in there, do you?"

"Me? Heavens, no."

"Well, Miss Eveline don't take too well to mothers trying to get their babies back. Three months ago, this wild woman came into that there orphanage in a rage, screaming at Miss Eveline 'bout wanting her baby back. Miss Eveline had to call Johnny Lee – that our sheriff. She caused quite a ruckus."

"Well, the truth is, I'm looking for a job."

"Uh huh." Ethel looked me up and down, taking in my expensive new clothes, and looked a little skeptical. "Well, Miss Eveline don't pay much."

I finished my sandwich and felt a little queasy every time I looked at those greasy fries. Ethel sat quietly, studying me. I could feel her searching for answers in my face.

"How much do I owe you?" I asked her.

"Buck-fifty."

I paid her with two ones and left. I felt all eyes following me. As I stepped over the railroad tracks, I knew without looking that every one of those customers was at the window watching my every move.

The old antebellum home had been converted into an orphanage. The once-wealthy landowner was long since passed away. It needed painting and repairs. It was obvious it had been neglected. I hoped the children weren't as neglected as the building they lived in.

The large, brass knocker felt hot from the sun as I rapped it against the huge door. The paint on the door was dingy and peeling, and the wood was chipped. I could hear the sound of the knocker echo inside.

A short, round woman opened the door. She couldn't have been more than four feet, five inches tall, and must have weighed about three hundred pounds.

"Miss Eveline?" I asked, and she nodded, looking a little cautious.

She had rosy cheeks, huge brown eyes, and a beautiful smile, but she looked tired. Her dress was homemade, and it had small flowers on a white background. Her hair was tousled, partly up and partly down, but it was a striking auburn color, and the white streaks in it shone in the sun. I guessed she must be nearly fifty.

"I understand you have a position open."

"It don't pay much," she said.

"That's fine. When do I start?"

"Don't you care it don't pay much?" she asked, surprised.

"Oh, yes, I need money, let me assure you. But I also need a job."

"You start in the morning for twenty-five dollars a week. Wear comfortable shoes."

It was my turn to be surprised. "Don't you want to see a resume?" I asked. "Don't you have a form I have to fill out?"

She shook her head. "I'll know within a day or two whether you're good with young'uns. That's all I care about."

"Thank you, Miss Eveline. I will be here at eight tomorrow morning."

"You have a place to stay?"

"No ma'am."

"See Jane Tudor. Sometimes she takes in boarders. Tell her you work for me."

"Yes, ma'am, I will. How do I find her?"

"Just ask anybody," Miss Eveline said as she closed the huge, wooden door.

I walked back to the hotel, undressed, and went to bed. I was exhausted. My thoughts drifted to my misses. She was dead and buried. Her daughter, Mister Joe's daughter, might be in that orphanage. I had no idea what was next. I decided to just see it through and hope for the best.

CHAPTER FIVE

I had my one schoolmarm dress left from where Mister Joe had taken me to the dress shops. I'm not sure why I kept it, but my new clothes were too dressy, so I put on the oversized dress and my army boots, as Peter Wilson called them. As my suitcase lay open on my bed, I remembered Mister Joe had told me he had placed his phone number in the silk inner pocket. The silk felt good against my hand as I felt around looking for his number. I understood now why the misses liked soft and fancy clothes against her body. I pulled out the folded piece of paper. Mister Joe had written:

Beth, you are a saint putting up with the misses. Her fits of anger drove me away from her. I miss her. She was the only woman I ever loved. My heart aches. My phone number is Andrew 6584. Call me any time. I seldom sleep.
Joe.

By the time I had gotten to the end of his note, my eyes were full of tears. A love so deep, so much a part of a person, it must have hurt terribly to lose her. Sometimes I wondered if I loved her or hated her. There were times I felt nothing. She was a great person most all of the time, until she had her episodes of strange behavior, talking out loud to no one, standing in front of that living room mirror, totally naked, her calamine baths, and her obsession with limes. It was all like a distant dream, a dream I chose to forget. I wanted to remember the good times, the times we laughed and acted like sisters and told each other everything.

Lord, the stories that woman could tell! She loved life and took everything she wanted from it. There was no doubt in my mind she would never end it, not on her own, not like that. Maybe her death was an accident. I couldn't help but wonder what happened in that bedroom after Peter Wilson arrived.

The early morning sun beat down on my drab, gray dress. As I walked by the diner, all eyes were on me. I paid them no attention, held my head up high, and focused on getting to the orphanage.

As I took the huge brass knocker in my hand, the door flew open. A small boy of about six grinned, showing several missing teeth, and said,

"Who are you?"

"I'm your new schoolteacher."

"Ah, I thought you was supposed to come adopt one of us." Disappointment showed on his face and could be heard in his voice.

"No, child. I'm here to prepare you for that day when someone comes here to adopt you. May I come in?"

"Yeah, I guess so." He scrambled up the old Victorian staircase.

Miss Eveline stood nearby eyeing my dress. "Good morning," she said.

"Oh, these are my normal work clothes. I hope you don't mind."

"I don't mind. I just hope you don't scare the kids with that get-up."

"All I have is my other suit I had on yesterday," I lied. "I can go put it on if you'd like that better."

"No, you are okay, I guess. It's just that you kind of surprised me. You looked so nice yesterday. I had hoped you would add a little color around here."

"Well, maybe after my first paycheck I can buy something a little brighter."

"Yeah, and a lot less spooky," she said flatly.

She turned and shouted over her shoulder: "Come this way. I have coffee. I want to get to know who works for me."

We sat and talked for hours. The kids played and, since there were no babies, we were pretty much uninterrupted. She was a fascinating woman. The mansion was her old home place. She never married; she had quit school in the eighth grade to help out at home. The once-wealthy family fell on bad times after the stock crash. Miss Eveline started working for the state of Tennessee by taking in orphans and kids with abusive parents. That evolved into her orphanage. I couldn't believe I was so relaxed with her. Her Southern charm was intoxicating. She made me feel as if we had been friends for years and were simply catching up on each other.

"I grew up in a small California town; the only industry there was fishing," I told her. "My dad was a fisherman and always smelled of fish. My mom had sixteen kids. I was the third born. Our small home was crowded, and food was scarce. As my older brothers and sisters came of age, they all went to work, bringing Mama their paycheck each Friday afternoon. There still wasn't enough money to keep us afloat. Then Dad had his fishing accident and lost an arm in a battle with a shark. They were sadly and desperately poor before the accident. Things only got worse. The best way I could help them was to leave. I was one less mouth to feed.

"I took a bus to Los Angeles. I had no money and no job. I found an old newspaper on a bus stop bench and started walking, applying for jobs listed in the newspaper. The misses' address was the eighth place I walked. She was, I guess, about six miles from the last place I had applied. It was getting dark. I was tired and hungry when I got to her home.

It was beautiful. It was the fanciest place I had ever seen. She had running water and a bathroom inside and heat and air conditioning. It was comfortable in her home."

The missus had hired me on the spot, I explained to Miss Eveline. Maybe she felt sorry for me, or maybe because she had been through so many housekeepers, she was desperate. I was never sure. She insisted I take a milk bath, and she gave me some old clothes of hers to wear for the evening.

"I made homemade biscuits and gravy, along with a small roast, carrots, potatoes, and such," I said, continuing my story. "I had never seen a pantry – a special room for food to be stored in! It was full and had more in it than the local grocery store I grew up close to. The next day she took me and bought me all gray dresses and strange shoes. I had to wear my hair in a bun. She insisted. Everything was great for a few months and then her fits started. I was scared to death she was going to hurt me. Some nights I slept in my small bedroom with the door locked. I eventually figured out about when they were going to happen and found a pattern. I learned to live with it. She died a few weeks ago."

Miss Eveline seemed fascinated with my story. She asked so many questions, and the last was, "Well, dear, that explains a lot, except one thing: How did that bring you here?"

My mind raced trying to figure out a lie that didn't sound like a lie.

"Oh, well, I got on a bus and just rode. When it stopped in Chattanooga, it looked so warm and friendly, I just got off the bus and stayed."

"I see," Miss Eveline said with a lot of doubt in her voice.

As the kids played and ran through the kitchen, I watched for a little girl of about four that looked like Mister Joe and the missus.

"How many kids do we have?" I asked in hopes of finding out some information about the girl without causing Miss Eveline to get suspicious.

"Right now we have four boys, age's five to nine, and four girls, ages' three to nine. They are getting age on them and are less likely to be adopted. Folks always want a newborn. Except one. I got this one newborn years ago and no one wanted her. She truly is a sad one. She seldom talks, always looks pouty and moody. I just have no idea what will become of her."

"Really? What's her name?"

"I named her Olivia. She got here when she was about three days old. When I first saw her, all small and sickly, I knew most folks wouldn't want her. Seems I was right. Too right. She is still here after four years."

My heart leapt. Maybe, just maybe I had found the child I was seeking. Olivia – I liked her name. Mister Joe would like it, too, I thought.

"Has Olivia come through? I haven't seen a child like you just described."

"Lord child, no. That girl sulks all day long in her room. She never leaves her room. We have tried getting her outside – you know a little sunshine is good for you – but she refuses to leave her room."

"Do you take her dinner up to her?"

"No, she does come down to eat, but she is so quiet, you would never know she is here. I have looked around, her plate is half eaten, and she is gone. Spooky quiet, that one. I can't help but wonder if she is maybe a little retarded or something, you know?"

"Well, I want to meet them all. Olivia, if you don't mind, can be my project. I would like to work with her after my chores are done."

"I can tell you now, you can't get through to her. She will break your heart."

"Oh, I don't mind."

"Okay, you can meet the others later. I will take you to Olivia's room. Finding her is never a problem." Miss Eveline took our coffee cups and placed them in the sink. She hesitated, standing at the sink. I couldn't help but wonder if she thought I was maybe Olivia's mother. She confirmed my suspicion seconds later.

"You don't have no kids of your own, do you?" she demanded.

"No, ma'am. I've never been married."

"Child, that don't count for nothing. The question was do you have any children of your own."

"No."

As I followed Miss Eveline up the huge, graceful staircase, she grunted and pulled on the banister. I knew then she didn't climb the steps much. That could only mean one thing. If Olivia seldom came down and Miss Eveline seldom went up, Olivia got very little attention.

As we walked down the corridor, Miss Eveline pointed out the children's bedrooms.

"Two boys sleep here; two girls sleep here," she said. Then we came to Olivia's room.

"She can't sleep with someone else in her room. She has to sleep alone," Miss Eveline said.

My heart broke for the child, neglected because she was quiet. How sad. I couldn't blame her for wanting her own room.

When Miss Eveline opened the door, I saw the room was drab and dark. Despite the heat outside, it felt cold and musty in there. The light from the hallway fell across the room. One small rocking chair sat next to the window. The saddest child I have ever seen sat in a worn, red rocker looking out the window. She was barely three feet tall, thin, and frail looking. She was pale, and those sad blue eyes would rip a mother's heart out. Her plaid dress was too big; her sandy brown hair was tangled and matted. She never looked up when we walked into the room. Her eyes were fixed on the kids playing outdoors.

I walked over and knelt between her and the window.

"Hello, my name is Beth," I said softly. "You can call me Miss Beth. And what is your name?"

The child sat there and stared at my left ear. Her tiny hands held tightly to the arms of her small, red rocker. Her bare feet looked cold and blue. Her toenails had not been trimmed in some time. My eyes wandered up to those tiny, hands and then to her hair. It would have to be cut off. It was far too tangled to ever run a brush through it.

"Say hello to Miss Beth, Olivia," Eveline demanded.

She drew her tiny feet up to her body as she mumbled words that were not understandable. She never raised her head.

"Well, Beth, are you ready to meet the rest of the kids?" Miss Eveline asked.

"Yes, of course."

I leaned over and lightly kissed Olivia on her left cheek. She didn't seem to notice. But as I started to turn away, I saw one small tear roll down her cheek. That's when I knew.

CHAPTER SIX

The next few weeks rushed by. It was mid-summer, and the heat was at its worst. July can be brutal in Ooltawah, Tennessee. No rain, no clouds, just hot, humid, heavy air that could make you feel as though someone was standing on your chest. There was no escaping the heat, except in Olivia's room. It was so odd. Her room was always cool.
I had made no progress with her as far as I could tell the first few weeks. She remained in her unresponsive state until the end of July. On July 30, something changed.

Her beautiful blue eyes actually caught mine in a stare. That was the first time I felt she actually connected with me. I read to her every afternoon as the other children played outside. She sat in her rocker and watched them play. I could only hope she was listening to the stories of Greek mythology I was reading to her. The kids back at my parent's home had loved hearing about the exploits of the gods and the humans they tormented or helped, depending on their dispositions and moods.

I read to her about Ares, the god of war, who was stuffed into a jar by two angry giants. I read stories about Aphrodite, goddess of love and protector of sailors, who was created from sea foam and wore a magic girdle that could make any man fall in love with her. I told her about Zeus, the Supreme Being on Olympus, who fought his father to save his siblings. And all the time, she just stared out the window. I marked my place in the aged book with Mister Joe's baseball card. Seeing his face gave me strength.

Each day after I read to her, I clipped a bit more hair off. The kids made fun of her hair, as it got shorter and shorter. She never reacted to their jeering. I bought her a silver brush and began brushing her hair as I read to her, propping the book up in the window. I always gave her a light kiss on the cheek after I brushed her hair.

Then, in August, when I came into her room to read, she turned away from the window and

watched me as I sat quietly next to her. She leaned back as I brushed her hair.
I made my first real breakthrough near the end of the month.

At my usual reading time, I had to attend to one of the children, who had fallen and needed a bandage and a hug. Kevin was a brave little soldier, always into something. He had jumped out of a swing, trying to fly, and skinned his knees and the palms of his hands.

Olivia came into the kitchen and watched as I gave Kevin first aid. She stood there looking down, sneaking peeks out of the corner of her eye. I saw her lean out of her wooden kitchen chair and stare at a large grandfather clock. It was just after one o'clock. I understood what was happening, and I was overjoyed. One o'clock, our usual reading time, had come, and gone, so she had come to find me. She was waiting for me to read to her. After I got Kevin taken care of, I took her small hand in mine and we climbed the stairs to her room. I read a little extra that day.

A week later, it occurred to me that if she came looking for me to read to her, then it was time I made her come find me outside. At a quarter to one, I sat under a huge pecan tree in the yard. The other children played around me, and I knew she was watching from her window. I began reading at exactly one o'clock. I could hear the grandfather clock striking in the living room. You could hear that clock three miles down the road.

Fifteen minutes later, Olivia walked outside. The kids jeered and hollered because it was such an event. She pushed her way through them and walked up to me. Her eyes locked onto mine. She turned away from me, and I thought she was going back upstairs. She surprised me with a butt flop squarely onto my lap. I immediately began reading.

She turned her body toward me, placed her hand over my mouth, and said, "Zeus." She wanted to hear a story about Zeus! I had trouble seeing the words on the page through my tears. The screaming children settled down as I began reading. Most sat nearby and listened to the story of Zeus. They were spellbound. Olivia leaned back against my chest. I had to readjust the book as I took one hand and stroked her hair.

The awful summer heat began to pass in September, so I often read to the children beneath the shade of the pecan tree.

On October 12, she turned five. She had lost so much of her sadness. She was bright, I could tell, and had learned more about Greek mythology than any other child in the orphanage. Her favorite of the mythical gods was Zeus. She could almost quote the story, word for word. She loved tales of Apollo, Hermes, and Poseidon. Just after her birthday she began asking questions about the gods, like why we never see them. She talked more and more, and like a normal child and began asking question after question.

Miss Eveline was astonished at the change in the Olivia. She told me something that evening that jarred me to the core, as I was about to walk back to Jane Tudor's rooming house.

"You know you have made such incredible progress with Olivia, I think someone may adopt her now."

Those words terrified me. I had grown to love Olivia as if she were my own child. I couldn't stand the thought of someone else adopting her. The possibility had just never occurred to me.

As I walked into the rooming house, Miss Jane met me at the door.

"Dinner in thirty minutes," she said. It was a ritual of hers. She hated eating alone. Since her unmarried sister passed away a few years ago, she had rented out a room that used to be her brother's. He was in New York and a major topic of conversation. She talked about him - and anything else that came to her mind - throughout the meal. Being alone all day, every day, will do that to you. I wasn't much company to her that night. I was upset at the thought of Olivia being adopted. In the nine and a half months I had been at the orphanage, seven kids had been adopted. Miss Eveline told me a child was adopted every month or so, as a rule, and was replaced by another child.

I was lost in thought and didn't notice Miss Jane had stopped talking until she touched my hand.

"Honey, you deep into thought, now aren't you? I tried to tell you a few times, there is a letter from your mama on your dresser."

I excused myself, and went to my room. I opened the letter as I sat on the bed's edge and read the letter:

Dear Elizabeth,
Your dad passed away. Please come home when you can. He was buried last Wednesday.
Love, Mother

I crumpled the letter in my fist, lay back on the bed, and cried myself to sleep.
The next day, I told Miss Eveline I had to return to my hometown and see about my family.

She offered her sympathies, and then said, "Miss Beth, I been meaning to ask you something. You told me that first day that you took a bus and just wandered around with no place in mind. You saw Chattanooga, got off the bus, and stayed."

"Yes."

"Well, child, I like you, I swear I do. You are a great help and the kids love you, especially Olivia, but for the life of me I can't figure out why you felt the need to tell me such a story. I knew all along, before you got to my door, that you flew into Chattanooga. Jake is my nephew. You know, that crazy taxi driver that delivered you from the airport."

I tried for a minute to think of another lie to make the first one seem more plausible, but when I saw the look on her face, I knew she would not be fooled by anything I could come up with.

"Well, if I told you why I was really here, I thought you would boot me out."

"And why are you really here?" She didn't seem angry, but I knew she would not tolerate less than the truth.

"I'm sworn to secrecy, Miss Eveline. It's not to hurt anybody or anything like that."

"It has something to do with Olivia, doesn't it?"

"Yes, ma'am, it does. I suppose I'm sworn to secrecy to only one man. If he ever found out, I would lose all that I have."

"And what exactly do you have?"

"I was left with a lot of money and told to keep an eye on Olivia."

"I see."

"Child, you lied before. Why should I believe you now?"

"Miss Eveline, I am convinced Olivia is my former employer's baby girl."

"You mean that lady actor?"

"Yes, ma'am. She left me a lot of money and told me as long as I don't tell whom the mother and father are, I can keep the money. My family needs that money, Miss Eveline. I have brothers and sisters at home, and they have no daddy to take care of them. My mother can't take care of them by herself. They have no money to survive on."

She patted my arm and smiled.

"Child, that woman left you in a pickle. You won't have to worry about me telling anyone. Your secret is safe with me. Are you coming back?"

"Well, Miss Eveline, I'm not sure what I will find in California. It depends on whether my family needs me or not."

"What about you having to look after Olivia?"

"Well, in her will she didn't say I had to do anything special. Just look out for her is all the will reads. The big thing is for the daddy not to find out about her."

"I see. Well, you go see about your family. I will take good care of Olivia. That child, I swear, she wants me to read that mythology book to her any time you aren't around. That book belonged to my great-granddaddy. I don't think anyone, including him, ever read it before. I just can't imagine a child being so wrapped up in a book that most adults won't read."

"Miss Eveline, it's her connection to this world. The stories give her hope."

"I guess that makes sense. Now go, do whatever you need to do, and get back here. Girl, you have to know I sure am going to miss you."

I had to talk around a lump in my throat that I couldn't seem to swallow. "I will miss you and all the kids."

"Olivia will be fine. Now go on before she hunts you down for another story reading session." Miss Eveline turned me toward the door and gave a light nudge. I turned and hugged her and rushed up the stairs. Olivia was asleep. I didn't disturb her.

I had everything packed and ready to go in just a few minutes. I kept life simple, and all I owned was the wardrobe Mister Joe had helped me pick and a few colorful dresses I bought in Ooltewah's Women's Fine Fashions on Main Street.

Jake tooted his horn. The whole town knew I was going back to California to see my family. I was surprised when I saw that a lot of them stood out in the road and waved goodbye. Small towns - everyone knows everyone else's business. I loved it.

The ticket man took some travelers checks for my ticket back to Los Angeles. As I boarded the airplane, ducking to clear the doorway, my heart ached. What if Olivia was adopted while I was gone? As I sat in my seat, I dug through my purse, looking for Mister Joe's phone number. I held it in my hand for the entire trip. Once I made the connection in Atlanta, I fell asleep, dreaming of Olivia, Mister Joe, and my misses.

They could have been a perfect family - a child in need of love, a mother who also needed love, and a father who had so much love to give. It was too late for the misses, and the other two didn't know about each other.

If I had known I would not see Olivia for another thirteen years, I would never have gotten on the plane.

CHAPTER SEVEN

As soon as I landed, I called Mister Joe.

"Mister Joe?"

"Beth!" Mister Joe, boomed as if I were an old friend.

"Mister Joe, can we meet? I mean, are you busy or something?"

I told him where I was, and he said he'd meet me there in thirty minutes.

I walked around wringing my hands. I had no idea what to say. If I should tell him, what would Keyes and Ottoman do to me? I felt dizzy as I thought of all the possibilities. I couldn't sit still, so I paced.

As I turned toward the door at the front of the airport terminal, I saw him coming toward me. He was nearly running, and he was wearing a smile as broad as the Mississippi. He scooped me up in his arms and spun around twice. He took my breath away.

"God, I've missed you!" he hollered loud enough for everyone in the vicinity to hear.

"Why, thank you, Mister Joe," I said as he gently put me down. He was so strong, but he managed to be gentle. My heart pounded.

"I'm glad you're home. How was your visit?" he asked as he took my right hand and led me towards the door. My heavy suitcase was nothing to him. He swung it forward a time or to, like a schoolboy. His grip on my hand was firm, as if he intended to never let go again. He made me feel safe.

He held the car door open for me and tossed my suitcase in the back seat. The top of his beautiful, baby blue Thunderbird convertible was down, and we drove toward the open road.

"Mister Joe, I have so much to tell you," I said.

"Later," he said in a tone that said he would hear no arguments. "Right now we are going for a bite to eat, then a drive, then a movie, then to my home. I'm not letting you out of my sight again."

I felt my face go red, and my heart raced.

"Mister Joe..."

"No, I'm not listening to any arguments."

"But, Mister Joe..."

"No buts, Beth, so you might just as well relax and enjoy."

When we walked into the restaurant he had chosen, he took my right hand, pulled it through his left arm, and locked on to me. He strolled through the restaurant as if he was a king and I was his queen. If he had looked at my face, he would have seen fear and shock. But he was too busy nodding at his buddies.

The waiter led us to a quiet, candlelit booth. As we settled in, Mister Joe finally looked me in the eye, and for the first time, he saw my fear.

"What?" he demanded.

"Mister Joe, I been trying to tell you, my dad passed away. My family needs me."

"I'm sorry. We will drive down this afternoon. But for now, you are all mine."

His? I couldn't believe my ears. He had been married to one of the most beautiful women in the world. He couldn't possibly mean he wanted me.

"Now tell me what's going on with your family," he said after he ordered two dry martinis.

"Mister Joe, you know I have never had a drink."

"That changes today, baby. Now tell me your news," he said, putting his hand gently on mine.

"It's my dad, Mister Joe. He passed away last week. My family is very poor."

"You got plenty of money; give them some," he said as if that settled everything.

"Look, Mister Joe, slow down. Listen to me."

"Sure, sweets, go ahead." He smiled so big I could count his teeth.

"Mister Joe, I found a little girl."

"Was she lost?"

"Oh, yes, she was very lost."

"And?" Mister Joe motioned impatiently with his left hand for more information.

"Mister Joe, it's complicated."

"Why? Is she yours?"

"No, but I love her all the same, as if she was mine."

"Okay, we will go get her."

"No, Mister Joe, we won't. The first thing I have to do is see to my family."

"Okay, we will eat, then drive down. I have great news for you."

"You do?"

Maybe that's why he is so animated and full of life, I thought. I had never seen him so excited, even when he was married to the misses.

"Look, after you left, I got to thinking: That savings account interest of two percent would have taken years to mature to any real money, so I had my broker invest two hundred grand for you."

"Is that safe?"

"Honey, not only is it safe, but you made that back plus more. He has taken your two hundred grand and turned it into eight."

"In ten months?"

"Oh, yeah, relax. He told me in one more month your initial two hundred grand would grow to one million. Honey, you are a millionaire!"

"Oh, Mister Joe, that's wonderful!" And then I realized I might still lose it all if I told him about his child. "I think it's wonderful," I added.

"What do you mean, you think? I thought you would be happy."

"Well, of course I am, Mister Joe. But let me ask you something: Suppose that money had a stipulation and I broke it?"

He frowned. "Then I imagine you would lose it all, including any profits. Did she have stipulations? And did you break them?"

"Yes and no, Mister Joe." I saw his frown deepen, so I added, "Yes, there were stipulations, and no, I haven't broken them."

"Then there's no problem. I bet Ottoman would be sad to know you didn't break them. That snake wants your money, you know."

"Yes, I know," I said. Before he could question me anymore, I changed the subject. "Mister Joe, when we leave here, I need to go to the bank and get money for my family."

"Sure, we can do that." Mister Joe said as he handed back the menu to our waiter. He ordered for both of us. I have no idea what I ate, but it was good. We were soon on the road to my small Southern California home. It had been almost ten years since I had been back. Every week, I had mailed half of my wages to mama. Since the missus paid me so little, it wasn't much. I was scared to spend what the misses left me. I didn't know when that nasty lawyer would come after my money and demand more, so I spent very little.

The nasty little village was worse than I remembered. It reeked of fish. The small house I grew up in was in worse repair than I remembered. Just looking at it made me want to bathe. Mister Joe took care of all the details. Within a few days, Mama and the three youngest kids had moved to a suburb twenty minutes south of Los Angeles. Mister Joe and I stayed at a local motel. It was drab, but I made do. I'm sure Mister Joe was uncomfortable in his motel room. He's used to only the best. After Mister Joe found them a house, and he insisted they all leave whatever was in the old house except personal items. No one argued, especially Mama. She gathered her pictures - there were only a few - and a few treasured mementos. The rest stayed behind.

Then, Mister Joe piled everyone into his convertible, and we drove to a furniture store. Mama couldn't believe her eyes. She couldn't stop crying. The delivery truck was parked for the day, but Mister Joe's persistence and his fame won the storeowner over. Before they knew it, Mama and the kids were settled in a new home with new furniture. Only Mister Joe could have pulled that off. I left Mama with fifty thousand in cash, and I had only spent twenty-nine thousand on the house and furniture. When we left them, the three boys were piled up in the living room floor, afraid to sit on the new furniture, watching a black and white TV. They were spellbound. Mama was still crying when we drove away late that night. Mister Joe made a call after we left and had five hundred dollars' worth of groceries delivered to their new home.

We were exhausted. It hadn't occurred to me that I had not secured a hotel room until I got back to the city with Mister Joe. I thought about staying with Mama and the boys, but Mister Joe wouldn't hear of it. It was almost midnight when we pulled up in Mister Joe's driveway.

When we got to his front door, he leaned over, opened the front door, and scooped me off my feet, cradling me like I was a baby. I was too tired to do anything but rest my head against his massive chest. I closed my eyes and felt like I was in the arms of Zeus, himself.

I tried not to think of the little girl I had left behind.

We ate sandwiches from the fridge and drank cold martinis. Before I knew it, I was in a huge tub filled with bubbles soaking my sore muscles and aching feet. I was totally relaxed. Mister Joe turned on a stereo nearby, and I could hear Elvis asking, *"Are you lonesome tonight?"* I was feeling the martinis, and I answered the question aloud: "I have been lonesome a lot of nights, Elvis." And I started to giggle.

Mister Joe walked in the bathroom wearing only a towel wrapped around his waist and a smile that spelled trouble.

I sat up, covering my breasts with my arms. "Mister Joe, we can't!"

"Oh, but we can," he said softly.

I had to remind myself this man didn't hear "no" very often. He could have anything – or anybody – he wanted. He had no idea how badly I wanted him, but this just couldn't happen. There were too many differences – and one large secret – between us.

He dropped his towel and stepped into the tub. I turned my head away. I felt my body quiver. I made room for him in the tub. He sat behind me and cradled me between his legs. He sipped on a martini he brought with him and then offered the glass to me. I gulped the whole thing down. He laughed.

Women weren't supposed to be curious about a man's naked body. Men were supposed to want sex, and women were supposed to submit. But a woman didn't explore a man's body, and women didn't enjoy sex. That was what my mama had taught me.

So I sat stiffly in the tub, my hands still hiding my chest, thinking if I were a good girl, I'd slap his face and run from the room. But I didn't really want to do that. I wanted to go on feeling his body pressed against me. He kissed the back of my neck and my shoulders, and his tongue slid down my back. His eyes traced every curve of my body and explored my mystery.

"You are beautiful," he said, as he reached for me.

I stepped out of the tub, but I didn't cover myself.

"Mister Joe," I whispered, "I'm a virgin. I want you badly, but the first time you make love to me, I want to be in your bed."

"I'm your first?" he asked, and I nodded.

He stood as the foam slid down his massive, muscular body, and I looked at him without shame.

"Mister Joe, please be gentle and patient."
"My love, I wouldn't have it any other way.

As he moved to lie beside me and wrapped his arms around me, I heard him whisper, "I knew it."

CHAPTER EIGHT

"Knew what?" I asked.

He chuckled, so I asked again, nudging him this time. "You knew what?"

He turned to face me. "I knew you were all I wanted and needed. I want to marry you."

"I have other obligations, Joe."

"Yeah, we both do, but we can work this out."

We were married three days later. Joe bought us a two hundred acre ranch two hours south of Los Angeles.

Over the next thirteen years, only one thing kept me from being totally happy: the guilt of leaving Olivia behind. But I knew I could not have the child and the man I loved, and I could not live without the man. So I tried to push Olivia from my mind. Once a year, I got a letter from Miss Eveline telling me of Olivia. After I left, Olivia retreated into her shell for a while, but as she got older, she became beautiful and more confident. By the time she was sixteen, she was stunning, Miss Eveline told me, bright and outgoing. Miss Eveline ended one of her annual letters with, "Oh, by the way, remember that dusty old mythology book? Well Olivia has not put it down since she was five."

The last letter from Miss Eveline bothered me more than any she had sent before. Olivia was one month from her eighteenth birthday and had to leave the orphanage soon. I worried for her.

I sent Miss Eveline five thousand dollars and asked that she give it to Olivia to help her get started in her new life. Joe and I wanted children, but we gave up after a few years and were content to be with each other. He was almost twenty years older than me, and, at sixty-four, he was becoming an old man. For the first time, I began to wonder what my life would be like without him. But those thoughts were too painful, and I tried to keep them at bay.

I had never told Joe about Olivia, though I sometimes regretted that and wondered if I had done the right thing. After so many years of holding the secret I was now worried I would lose him if I did tell him. I never found any comfort on either side of that secret.

Just before Olivia's eighteenth birthday, I received a letter from Evelin, saying Olivia was coming to Los Angeles to live. She asked if I could meet her at the airport and gave me her flight information. I told Joe that a friend from Ooltawah was coming.

Three days later, I drove into the Los Angeles airport and waited. I held a sign up with Olivia's name on it. I wasn't sure, after thirteen years, I would recognize her but, as it turned out, I didn't need the sign. As she approached me, I recognized her. She had so much of both parents in her that she was easy to pick out.

Her long, shiny, brown hair, was sprinkled with golden highlights. Her face was stunning and had so many characteristics of her mother.

Her walk was just like her mom's, sensuous and bouncy. She was five feet one, and she couldn't have weighed more than a hundred and ten pounds. She was a striking young woman. As she walked toward me, I noticed that people stopped to stare at her. My eyes fell on her nose. Her daddy's nose.
I called her over and gave her a hug.

"Olivia, how wonderful to see you!" I said. "I'm a friend of Miss Eveline's."

"It's good to meet you," she said softly, with a distinct Southern drawl.

"Well, we have found you a job and a small studio apartment. Miss Eveline asked that I get you settled."

"You are so kind," she said.

I showed her the studio apartment I had picked for her and drove her to a men's clothing store I had invested in with a friend I met through Joe. I was a silent partner. Ann Hollis, was my partner and ran the shop. It was successful, and many famous men shopped at our store. Olivia and I invited Ann to join us for lunch. The three of us talked endlessly as if we were old friends. Olivia talked about Miss Eveline with such affection, as if she was talking about her mother, it caused me a pang of jealousy. I could have been her mother, I thought, had I not chosen to stay with Joe. But what choice did I have, really? I loved my husband more than life itself.

Olivia and Ann got along famously, and before we drove Ann back to work, they had set a time and place to meet. Ann was going to help her pick out some clothes. Olivia mentioned that Miss Eveline had given her money, and I knew I could never tell her it came from me. I was feeling more miserable – and, frankly, more jealous – by the moment.

I stayed with Olivia, four days and then drove back home to be with my Joe. I missed him so much, it seemed like four years. He had the cook prepare a special meal, and we sat on the patio next to the pool and enjoyed each other's company.

As the months passed, Ann and Olivia became close friends. Olivia, told Ann, everything. The men who came into the shop always made passes at Olivia. She giggled and sold her customers clothing they would probably never wear. Olivia was good at moving merchandise that wouldn't normally sell, and the store became even more profitable. Dozens of men asked her out. She turned them all down.

My weekly call from Ann, about the business included tales of the antics guys pulled trying to get Olivia to go out with them.

By the time Joe turned sixty-seven, his health was failing. I watched him get weaker. He spent the next few months in and out of the hospital with kidney failure caused by an infection.

I turned all my attention to Joe and didn't talk to Ann very often. The doctors finally got Joe well, but he was left weak and shaky. We went

back to the ranch, and he began an exercise program to regain his strength. It took a few months, but Joe was determined to get back to his regular weight. Six months later he was as strong as an ox.
When Joe's crisis had passed, I called Ann to see what was going on with the shop and of course Olivia. It had been four months since we talked. I missed hearing about the antics of would-be suitors.

Ann and I chatted for a while. I gave her a progress report on Joe, and she talked about the store. Profits were up thirty percent from last year.

"It's never been busier," she said. "I think our little Olivia has had a direct impact on sales." Ann giggled, and I could hear Olivia's laughter in the background. "And let's see," Ann continued, "two months ago, I invited Olivia to move in with me. My son went off to college and I was lonely. She is as much fun at home as she is at work. She is like the daughter I never had."

I felt my gut twist into a knot. Now there were two women who had become mother figures to Olivia. She should have been my daughter, I told myself bitterly. I should have adopted her when Joe and I found out we couldn't have children. But I was so afraid I would lose him. He would never forgive me for keeping his daughter a secret all these years. I'd rather die than lost my special Joe.

Ann kept chattering away. She couldn't know I was in agony. "Oh, yeah, Olivia met quite a character. He has definitely turned her head, a first for her. They have been out on three dates. The last date, he kissed her," Ann gushed. "Her first kiss!"

Ann went on and on about the drama of the first date, all that went wrong, and then talked endlessly about Olivia's description of her first kiss. I had to stop Ann's droning to find out about the boy. He was twenty-two, she said, a swimmer who had won a gold medal at the Olympics. His name was Eric Jacobi. He was quite the celebrity, Ann told me. He had a nice income through product endorsements. I had seen him on TV advertising breakfast cereal and exercise equipment. He was strikingly handsome, and he was Greek. Olivia called him her Adonis. He certainly had the chiseled body of an Adonis. I wasn't sure exactly how she would handle herself with her first boyfriend, and it worried me. But what say could I have in Olivia's life? I had put my own happiness with Joe over hers, and now I was paying the price.

Joe decided he felt so good he wanted to "do Europe." We left for a month-long tour. Paris, Rome, and Athens - we saw them all. I watched Joe carefully until he finally told me to stop fussing over him. He was fine, he said decisively. We flew back into New York at the end of March. While we waited for our flight to Los Angeles, I bought a newspaper to catch up on what had been happening in the good old U.S. On the celebrity page, I saw pictures of Eric and my Olivia. She was wearing a satin and lace-wedding gown, laughing standing next to Olivia was Miss Eveline. I felt sick.
I spent the next few months heartsick over the decision I had made to keep silent about the

child I found in the Tennessee orphanage. I had deprived my husband of his daughter; I had kept her from her father; and I would never have a child of my own to love.

I had ruined everything in my loyalty to my misses.

Ann called lamenting how much she missed Olivia, and she laughed when she told me how many hearts Olivia had broken when she got married. Ann said she seldom saw Olivia anymore, though they talked on the phone from time to time. I had finally accepted that she was married and my duty to her as assigned by the will, I thought, was complete. I could not have been more wrong.

Three years after their marriage, Eric and Olivia had two boys, Zeus and Apollo, and she was pregnant again. Eric wanted twenty children, Ann told me with a laugh. Olivia wanted a lot, but not quite that many, Ann said. I smiled when I heard she had named her sons, Zeus and Apollo. She still had the treasured book of Greek mythology I read to her as a small child. The book was a bridge between her withdrawn world and the active world she now lived in.

Joe was approaching seventy, and I was pushing into my mid-fifties. We were happy in our ranch love nest. Joe bred quarter horses and that kept him out from underfoot. He entered every quarter horse competition possible, and his den was filled with trophies and ribbons. He was sure proud of his horses.

The clothing store fell on bad times, and there wasn't enough profit to go around, so Ann bought me out. She did okay in her little shop as a single owner.

As the years passed, I made peace with the decision I had made so long ago to keep the misses' secret. Joe, at seventy-three, was in remarkable health, and at fifty-nine, I was energetic and happy. I had heard through Ann that Olivia had delivered triplets. She named them Hermes, Achilles, and Neptune. Ann and I laughed over the names.

Later, Olivia and Eric had twins, Midas and Mercury. Then came another son, Vulcan; then a son named Eros. She was pregnant again with their tenth son. Ann said they were going to name him Poseidon. Ten sons in nine years of marriage! I could only imagine what their household must be like. The next three years brought their two daughters, Artemis and Demeter.

Miss Eveline wrote frequently. She told me she had fainted when the triplets were born and again when the twins were born. The media occasionally ran pictures and updates on the family. Eric was still remembered for his Olympic triumph. Once I saw a picture of Miss Eveline holding one of the babies. The caption on the picture said "Proud Grandma." I cried all day after seeing that picture. It haunted my dreams.

Then I began to hear disturbing reports through the news media. The troubles began early on, after Zeus was born, I read. Olivia showed signs of exhaustion and had fits of anger. Eric and the housekeeper convinced themselves she was experiencing "mother's blues." By the time Demeter, the last daughter, was born, Eric wanted a divorce. He gave Olivia their huge home, a healthy monthly income, and anything else she wanted. He just wanted out.

I knew it was time for me to become involved in Olivia's life. I knew what had to be done.

I visited Olivia three days before Demeter's fourth birthday. Zeus was nineteen. The home was a mess. Clothes were strewn across the living room floor. The kitchen had not been cleaned in weeks. Dirty dishes and containers from take-out restaurants were everywhere. Joe was on a nationwide tour with his quarter horses. The timing was perfect.

I found a small thrift shop and bought seven drab, gray dresses and "army boots" like the ones my misses used to make me wear.

I applied in person for the housekeeper's position. The past twelve housekeepers had quit, none staying more than a week. As I sat in the nasty kitchen, my stomach turned. Zeus went in search of his mother. It was ten minutes before she finally trudged into the kitchen. It was obvious she had been sleeping. She was pale and tired-looking, and she had thrown on a white, terrycloth robe.

We hadn't seen each other in years, and she didn't recognize me. When I tried to tell her my qualifications for the job, she waved her hands to show her indifference and said, "Whatever."
"Just see if you can bring some order to the house for us," she said. "The kids are out of control. I have had to turn to Valium just to make it one day to the next. Start when you like."

She looked old and exhausted. Her mental state had always been fragile, like her mother's, and having so many children had made the situation worse. Her dependency on prescribed drugs made her listless and ineffective.

I started cleaning immediately. There were days I didn't see her. She stayed in her bedroom for a week or better at a time, only coming out occasionally to eat. The kids were left on their own. Their schoolwork suffered. I never saw Eric. He stayed away. The news reported that he was engaged to a New York woman, the heiress to a fortune made in the tobacco industry.

I worked hard in that huge house of Olivia's. I had my hands full with ill-tempered children and the chaos they caused. I wasn't sure I was up to the challenge. The changes that were needed were a lot deeper than the cleaning of a stove or refrigerator. I had to take full charge. I knew how the ranch had revived my Joe. I also knew the Los Angeles lifestyle was hurting the children's chances of being the kind of people I wanted them to be. They were disrespectful, spoiled, and lazy.

Olivia was in one of her stupors when an attorney stopped by with papers to sell the house. I persuaded her to buy a hundred acres with an old farmhouse just outside Ooltawah,

Tennessee. I packed up those twelve kids and Olivia, and we moved there. I told Joe I was visiting an old friend in Ooltawah and left a number where he could reach me.

It was the best thing I could have done for my lost Olivia and her children. The kids were angry and resentful at first, but they soon discovered they loved the woods, and gardening, and caring for animals. At times, Olivia didn't even realize she had left Los Angeles. Pills and booze kept her in a stupor.

Miss Eveline had retired from her orphanage and moved in with us. She and I had a lot of work to do to make this family whole again.

Once we were settled, I hired someone to build a baseball park in the side yard, floodlights, and all. I bought ten baseball rulebooks and gave each boy his own copy. The local store ran out of baseball equipment and had to order bats and gloves and balls for the boys. Miss Eveline and I had the boys under control and focused on baseball. Though they couldn't know it, they had a love

of baseball in their genes, and they needed something to burn up their youthful energy. Harry, Jane Tudor's brother had coached major league baseball before retiring eight years ago. He longed for a challenge and the boys were definitely that.
The two baby girls watched and cheered every afternoon on a blanket under an old oak tree. Olivia never came outside, but she watched her boys play ball from her second story window in a rocking chair that she insisted be painted red.

Harry Tudor donned his baseball uniform, his belly hanging over his trousers, and came to meet the boys. The boys laughed at him at first, but he got their attention by making them run laps around the field.

The boys attended Ooltawah School. The town had grown so much from the time I had lived here. The diner was gone and the old stores had been replaced with newer, modern stores. Downtown had gone through a major revitalization. It was a beautiful small town. The mayor was progressive and worked hard for his community. Born in Ooltawah, Ray Albright was the best thing Ooltawah had going for it.

It took Miss Eveline and me three months to get everything lined up and to get the kids settled down. The real work had just begun.

CHAPTER NINE

Joe had three more months on the road with his horses. We spoke most every night. I hoped I could accomplish my goals in only three more months.

Coach Tudor came by every afternoon. If the boys were late for practice, they knew Coach Tudor would make them run laps. They quickly fell in line with his strong direction. Miss Eveline and I could see major changes in the boys' attitudes, even off the playing field. Coach Tudor drove those boys harder than he did the professional players, and they viewed him with affection and respect.

Zeus, now nearing twenty was a natural at baseball, Coach Tudor said. The other boys needed more help, he said, but they all showed a lot of natural ability.

"Miss Beth, I think we got us some raw talent here," he told me, "better than I've seen at the big show. I think you can just keep the money you offered to pay me to coach them. I think

I'll do it just for the love of the game. No offense, but you can use my salary to supply these boys with better equipment. What you bought them is second rate. Don't mean to insult you, ma'am, but that's about all the local store would carry. The expensive, better stuff wouldn't sell in a small town. If you don't object, I'll order what they need."

Then he added, "I have to tell you, I am amazed at the raw talent here. Have they ever played organized ball before?"

"No, Coach, the plain truth of it is, they were like young animals in their past environment. That's why I moved them here. I hoped you would be available to coach them. Miss Jane got all excited when I called her. I think you must be underfoot at home."

He laughed so hard, he doubled over, and he admitted I was probably right.
"Well, I can pass along what I know, but there will come a day, probably sooner than we want, that you will have to find another coach

who can take them further. And you say they never played any organized ball before?"

"No sir, the only thing organized in their lives was their home address. It was the only thing that didn't change daily."

"Well," he said, shaking his head in wonder, "that Zeus has some strong possibilities. I'm not joking when I tell you I had kids in the majors who would have killed for his abilities. Apollo is strong and fast for a nineteen-year-old. The triplets are dynamic, and the twins are going to be as good as Zeus, I believe. The younger boys show promise. It will be up to us to develop their talent."

"That's why we're here, Coach. We want those boys to have every chance in life. Had we left them where they were, they might not have made it to adulthood."

"Well, we can make do with the equipment you bought for a few weeks until the better stuff arrives. Meanwhile, I suggest you contact a carpenter."

"A carpenter? Why do we need a carpenter?" I asked.

"Ma'am, you will need bleachers. These boys are about to draw in the whole county with their ball playing. You will need a place for them to sit."

Coach Tudor drew up his roster. He wanted Zeus as pitcher, Apollo as catcher, the triplets on each base, Midas at short-stop, his twin Mercury at center field, Vulcan at right field, and Eros at left field. Poseidon, the youngest, had no position, so Coach Tudor decided he needed to learn all positions to fill in.

The next three months were focused on hard training. Zeus turned 21. Apollo was 20; Hermes, Achilles, and Apollo 19; Mercury and Midas 18, Vulcan was 17; Eros 16 and Poseidon 15.

Coach Tudor's practice sessions were rigorous, and sometimes a bit hard on young Poseidon, but they all persisted. After three hard months,

Coach Tudor felt the boys were ready for a little competition. Mayor Albright, recognizing an opportunity, invited the firemen from District 7 in Chattanooga in for a ballgame. District Seven's firefighters were known as the toughest ballplayers in Chattanooga. Some were good enough to make the Chattanooga Choo Choo's, a minor league that fed the New York Yankees.

Mayor Albright promoted the event himself. He invited the mayor of Chattanooga, Steve Wilson, and an avid baseball fan. Word of mouth did the rest. People from three counties drove in for the game. Coach Tudor was right; bleachers were indeed needed.

When the bus arrived with the firemen, the lumberjack-size men stepped off, laughing and joking about playing a bunch of kids. Coach Tudor believed they wouldn't be laughing when they left for home. He had a secret that no one else knew.

The boys decided they wanted to name their team after themselves, so they all wore "Jacobi" jerseys, and their numbers were assigned in order of their births. They were nervous, but Coach Tudor was confident.

More than a thousand people showed up. Some walked as far as two miles because parking was a problem. Mayor Albright assigned special seats for himself and his family. Albright also had seating for the Chattanooga's mayor and his family. The striped awning over their padded bleachers told the world they were dignitaries. Coach Tudor had Mayor Albright throw out the first ball.

Zeus took long, deep breaths. He talked quietly to his brothers and offered encouragement.

"Look, guys," he said, "If we fail today, we'll be laughed out of the county. I don't know how you feel, but I love it here. Our lives have never been better. Let's not blow this thing. Everybody just give your best."

Zeus reached out his right arm and Apollo put his hand over Zeus's. The triplets, then the twins, and then the other boys added their hands. Zeus shouted "and break" and the boys took their respective places on the field.

Zeus walked out to the pitcher's mound. He took a long, deep breath. The fireman at the plate was huge - six foot two, two hundred fifty pounds. He gripped his bat like he could slam a ball into the next county.

Zeus talked softly to himself. "I am named after the most powerful god. It is my job to see the other gods are taken care of. It is my job to lead them to victory. I can do this. Miss Beth believes in me, Miss Eveline believes in me, Coach Tudor believes in me, my brothers and sisters believe in me, and I believe in me. Now let's get this done."

Slowly, he raised his right foot off the mound and drew back with all the power and force he could muster. The ball went three feet over the batter's head. Apollo scrambled to return to ball. Before he pitched it back, Apollo gave Zeus the "calm down" sign. Zeus nodded.

The next ball hit Apollo's glove with a thud. The batter never saw it coming. Mayor Albright come up out of his seat and yelled, "Yeah!" The crowd roared.
The next two pitches went square down the middle, humming so fast the batter was left standing there looking confused.

Apollo heard the umpire say, "Son, that's all you get; three strikes, you are out." The crowd cheered.

The next two batters went the same way. Zeus threw his fastball straight down the middle; humming so fast the batters had no time to react. Coach Tudor's secret was out. Zeus was moving the ball at tremendous speed. No one knew how fast, but everyone knew it was so fast; it couldn't be seen or hit.

The brothers retired to their dugout. Coach Tudor was all over Zeus, patting him on the back. "Son, you stood up to the pressure. That is ninety-nine percent of the game, right there. It's all a mind game but you need talent and confidence. If you can do that a whole ballgame, you can take your game anywhere."

"Thank you, Coach," Zeus said, smiling broadly.

Coach Tudor had trouble deciding how to arrange the batting order. He took the easy road and stuck with the boys' numbering system. Zeus was up first.

If the crowd had loved his pitching, now they were about to see something truly spectacular. The fireman's pitcher decided he would play Zeus' game - heat down the middle. Zeus connected with the first pitch. The ball soared past the fence line and out of sight. Spectators jumped out of their lawn chairs and off their blankets and cheered as the ball sailed away. Zeus cleared the bases as spectators stomped and yelled and slapped each other on the back.

Everyone settled down as the run was posted on the manual scoreboard. Apollo walked up to the plate, braced his body, and waited for the first pitch. Coach Tudor whispered in his ear, “Low and inside.” That meant the ball would be coming at Apollo a lot slower than it had at Zeus. He was used to snagging fastballs.

When the fireman turned loose the ball, Apollo had to adjust to the slow pitch, but he got a large piece of it and sent it flying beyond the barbed-wire fence. Major Albright came up out of his seat again. The Chattanooga mayor sat still and covered his face with both hands. He mumbled, “Holy shit.”

Apollo zipped around the bases.

As Hermes stood to stretch, Coach Tudor said, “Take the first two pitches. Do not swing at the first or second ball.”

“Yes, sir,” the boy snapped, his eyes riveted on the pitcher. “That's right,” he mumbled aloud. “You saw my older brothers hit, but you haven't seen nothing yet. Come on with your best.”

The first two pitches were perfect strikes. Hermes was unfazed. He had been given his orders and wasn't about to challenge them. The third pitch was hard and down the middle. His bat cracked against the ball and it went over center field, well beyond the fence. The crowd went wild, and Mayor Albright once again came up out of his seat. He couldn't resist the temptation to give the Chattanooga mayor a little shove on the shoulder. Mayor Wilson wasn't amused.

Mayor Albright called one of his county engineers over and whispered in his ear. The man disappeared into the field and came back in a few minutes. He leaned over and talked quietly into Mayor Albright's ear. The mayor's eyes popped wide open, and a grin as big as the president's yacht spread across his face.

Achilles came up to bat. Coach Tudor said, "Son, the first pitch you get will be your best. Make the most of it."

"Yes, sir, Coach." The eighteen-year-old assumed the stance the coach had taught them all. "I love this game," Achilles thought to himself. "No one can hit this ball farther than I can. No one can run the bases as fast I can. And no one can throw a ball as far as I can. I am the best. It's time to prove it." As the fireman pitcher prepared to pitch, Apollo squatted into his power-hitting stance. He hit the ball with a thud, grunting. The ball sailed farther than any of the balls so far. Mayor Albright and his engineer knew, even if no one else did, those boys were hitting flight line drives down the middle consistently beyond six hundred feet.

Apollo ran the bases so fast; he made it back home before the ball bounced to a stop in a field. The engineer later measured the hit at six hundred thirty-five feet.
Mayor Albright's wife leaned toward the mayor. "Did you see how fast he ran the bases? No one can run the bases that fast!"

"Not now, dear. Not now," the mayor snapped.

It was Neptune's turn at bat. Of all the brothers, he was the calmest as he faced the pitcher. He didn't talk himself up. He squeezed his fingers tightly around the bat and waited. Coach Tudor knew he didn't need instructions on what ball to take. He knew Neptune had THE instinct.

The first pitch was low and outside. The second pitch was a heater down the center. Neptune connected, and as his ball sailed past the fence, Mayor Albright knew it flew more than six hundred feet. Neptune tagged all the bases and was back at home plate in fourteen seconds.

Mayor Wilson slumped in his chair. The firemen on the bench were quiet. The only hope they had now was, as the brothers got younger, maybe they couldn't hit as well, or maybe one would make a mistake. Eros strutted to the plate. He hit the ball just short of the barbed-wire fence.

The score was nine to nothing. The batting lineup started over with Zeus at bat. The city engineer stayed in center field and became the official distance guru. Zeus's ball fell about three feet short of six hundred and fifty; Apollo's was twenty feet short. Each time the boys whacked the ball, it went farther outfield.

On the third rotation, the firemen quit. They went home humiliated. Olivia cried Her eyes blurred by tears, she knew her boys had found their future.

Miss Eveline was amazed. "Harry," she said, "what did you put in those boys' heads? I've never seen any boy play ball like that before."

"Eveline, those boys are all naturals," the coach replied. "Damnedest thing I've ever seen. They play ball like Joe DiMaggio did in his prime."

I listened as the two chattered on. My boys were about to change baseball history. My plan was working. The only problem I could see was Joe was slated to be back home in two weeks. My job in Ooltawah wasn't close to finished.

Joe and I talked on the phone late that night. He missed me, and I certainly missed him. He gave me great news: His horses had placed first and second in most divisions, and he was invited to England to show his horses. He was, of course, delighted, but he was reluctant to leave me behind.

I invited Joe to the farm for the weekend, before he headed for England. I wanted so badly to tell Joe that he had a daughter and grandchildren. I knew I was taking a huge chance inviting him to the farm. I was afraid he might see himself or his lost love in the faces around him.

I was prepared to take that chance. I missed my husband, my own Zeus.

The mayor lingered after the game, slapped each of the brothers on the back, and told them all how proud he was. He had big plans for the brothers, he said. They could help him promote Ooltawah.

Mayor Wilson went back to Chattanooga and decided he would set up an all-star team from all divisions of firemen and policemen. Surely with an all-star team, he could find players to "whoop a bunch of kids," he said. He was embarrassed by the firemen's show and sought out the best players who worked for the city, no matter what department they worked in. In particular, he searched for a good pitcher. For the next two days, he conducted no city business. He was obsessed with finding a pitcher.
After the game was over, and the crowds were gone, the brothers sat at a special picnic table I had hired a local carpenter to build. It could accommodate all twelve children and two adults. The girls went inside with me and Miss Eveline.

Zeus had something to say, and his bothers listened closely.

"I have never been as proud of you guys as I was today. It's not that we beat the socks off those firemen. That isn't what happened today. Apollo, what do you think happened today?"

"Well, let's see. You pitched a no hitter and we all got home runs."
"Hermie, what did you observe from the day?" Zeus asked.

"Well, I think Apollo said it all."

" Achilles?"

"We slaughtered their butts."

The boys laughed and punched Achilles playfully on his shoulders.
"Tuneboy, what do you have to say?"

"We sunk their ship, Zeus. We simply outplayed them."

" A better answer. Midas? Mercury?"

"What everyone has said is true. I can't think of anything else," Mercury responded.

"Okay, Posey, can you explain to your older brothers exactly what happened here today?"

Poseidon looked thoughtful for a minute, then said, "Well, I didn't get to play. None of you got hurt, so I could watch you closely. I did see something that maybe no one else did. No one has mentioned it."

Zeus nodded. "Go ahead, Poseidon, teach your older brothers. Tell us what you understood from today."

"Well, you guys outplayed the other team, all grown men. That shows remarkable talent and strong aptitude for the game. What I think is we all found our destiny today."
Zeus jumped up and slapped his palms together. "Exactly!" he shouted. He grabbed Poseidon on each side of his face and kissed his forehead. "Little brother, you nailed it. Baseball is our future. It's why we are here. We have to get better and more refined. Did you notice how poised the firemen began? We were all nervous. I watched each of your lips move as you got up to bat. You were talking

yourself up. I did, too. But those firemen showed something we didn't: confidence. The more we play, the better we get, the more confidence we gain. Baseball is what, little brother?"

"A head game," Poseidon answered.

"That's it! Exactly! We let their size and age get into our heads. We can't let that happened to us again. Now, there's one other thing. That mayor from Chattanooga left here pissed. We beat his finest. Coach Tudor told me that we should prepare for an onslaught. That man went back to Chattanooga determined to find a team from his city that can beat us. We can't let that happen. We play his all-stars Saturday. That means what, little brother?"

Poseidon spoke up. "We got lots of work to do."

"Now, Coach will pull you out of the batter's box in a heartbeat if you hit anything except a high line drive down center, right?"

The boys nodded.

"That means we have to practice more, and maybe that means Coach Tudor ain't always here. But he gave us what we need, so let's work on what he gave us."

"Yeah, but he ran our butts off making us lap the bases. If we came in under fifteen seconds, we had to run for an hour. Heck, I would make the fifteen seconds just so I wouldn't have to do that hour of running. Nobody paid any attention to our running," Midas complained.

"True, they didn't, but the time will come when we will need that strength and speed. Coach Tudor knows what he is doing. He has made us the players that we are. It's up to us to make ourselves better. Besides, if we give any less, we disrespect Coach. No man has ever taken the time to forge us into anything worthwhile."

"Yeah, but we never even got to throw a ball. There were times I think I cried myself to sleep with my arm aching so badly from throwing so much," Mercury complained.

"That's true, too, Merc, but think of it like this: Coach prepared us for throwing. He says we can hum a ball better than any of his major leaguers. Know what that means? When we need it, the skill is there. When those batters figure out my pitching, they're going to get hits, and when they do, you guys have to get the ball to Apollo. Now for Eros and Vulcan, that may mean a throw of better than three hundred feet. What you guys need to focus on is four hundred feet, in the air and in Apollo's glove. That is where Coach Tudor is taking us, boys. But we have to develop, build, and focus."

Zeus stood and held out his right hand; the brothers stacked and broke on Zeus's command.

Coach Tudor was resting behind an old oak tree. He heard everything. Later that night, when we talked about what the boys had said, I could tell he was touched. What started out as something to do had turned into something that had to be. Fate was afoot.

CHAPTER TEN

Late that evening, Zeus decided to search the fridge for a snack. I sat quietly in the dark kitchen, enjoying the peace. I jumped as Zeus flipped on the light. He jumped when he saw me sitting at the kitchen table. After a moment of surprised silence, we both laughed.

"Come sit with me after you get something to eat," I said. "There's some of Miss Eveline's fried chicken left in there, I think."

Zeus fixed a quick plate and settled down across from me.

"You know, I was so proud of you boys today."

"Thank you Miss Beth," he mumbled around a mouthful of chicken. "We tried hard to beat those firemen. Man, those were some big fellas, weren't they?"

"You bet. They were some bruisers, all right. I kind of wondered if they just didn't take you boys seriously at first. Then they realized too late just how good you are."

"Yeah, I thought the same thing, Miss Beth. They sure didn't like getting skunked, did they?" Zeus's grin spread slowly across his face as if he was remembering the losers' faces.

"You have such a beautiful smile, Zeus."

"Thank you, Miss Beth."

"I've seen that smile before."

"Ma'am?"

"Oh, never mind. I'm just a silly old woman."

"No, ma'am, that's not true. You saved this family, Miss Beth. Mama up there isn't right, and the younger kids were turning into criminals. You saved our butts, is what you did. I just want you to know how grateful I am to you. It's like you knew all along exactly what to do and what we needed."

"Well, I don't know about all that, Zeus. But I do have to admit things are working out fairly well."

"Miss Beth, you're no housekeeper, are you?"

I had to fight off a feeling of panic. I hoped he hadn't seen the fear of being discovered in my eyes. "Whatever made you ask that question, son?"

"Miss Beth, a housekeeper doesn't wear three hundred dollar designer shoes."

I had given up the drab clothes and clunky shoes after several weeks with my new family. I thought no one had noticed or cared. I shifted uneasily in my chair while Zeus kept talking.

"Now me, I would have never noticed it, but you know Artemis reads herself to sleep each night with fashion magazines. She didn't put it together on her own. She just asked me how you could afford expensive shoes, clothes, and stuff. You know she notices stuff like that. I just figured you were an angel sent to watch after us."

His words brought me close to tears. "If you only knew, my sweet Zeus."

"Knew what?"

"How much I love each of you kids. How special you truly are."

"So, how did you afford such expensive clothes?"

"I inherited a lot of money, years ago, Zeus, and good investments turned it into a small fortune."

"Well, if you got all that money, why are you housekeeping?"

"Now that's a tougher question, Zeus." I knew lying to him would be wrong, and he would probably see right through me. But how could I possibly tell this youngster the truth?

Zeus ate two chicken breasts and was gnawing on the third. He dropped the third piece, half-eaten, into his plate and said, "Man, I ate too much." He paused for a moment and added, "What I should say is I talk too much. Look, I'm sorry if I made you uncomfortable. It just doesn't add up. I have to protect my family, Miss Beth. Everything you have done for us has been good, shoot, even great! But there must be something to this – all your money and you housekeeping."

"There is, Zeus. As a young woman, I found a job with Miss Eveline in her orphanage. That's where your mother grew up, you know."

"Mom grew up in an orphanage? She doesn't talk about her past much."

"Yes, she did. When I worked there, I got close to your mother. She was such a sweet child, and she needed loving care. Miss Eveline tried, but she had her hands full with a house full of kids. So I spent time with your mother. We grew close."

"What does that have to do with us kids?"

"A lot, Zeus. Your mother has problems. I surely don't have to tell you that. You kids needed help. So I jumped in, making you kids my business. Guess I meddled, and maybe I shouldn't have."

"Why do you say that, Miss Beth? Most of my brothers would be in jail by now, if you hadn't taken us out of the jungle. Here, we have had to depend on each other. We got closer, you know. They all hated it at first. They said you were going to turn us into a bunch of hicks."

"Hicks?" I had to laugh.

"Yes, ma'am, hicks. But you know, as we made it day by day, the folks around here were nice, calm, and friendly. I guess if that's a hick, we all choose to be hicks."

"I see. Then you kids are happy here?"

"You have done the right thing, Miss Beth. I told you that early on. There's more I need to tell you."

"What's that?" I asked as I placed my hand on Zeus's.

"Well, after the game, some dude from Chattanooga asked me to come to tryouts for the Chattanooga Choo Choos."

"And are you?"

"No, ma'am. Wouldn't think of it."

"Why?"

"Because we are a family, Miss Beth. We stick together, no matter what."

"Yes, but, Zeus, you could get a lot of play in with semi-pros as your brothers grow up. They are way too young to play semi-pro. Think of the experience, and what you could learn and bring home to them."

"Yes 'sum," he said. I smiled when I heard him say "yes 'sum" because I could see he was becoming more Southern by the day. Los Angeles was a distant memory, and not a particularly pleasant one for him.

"But," he went on, "we are one for all and all for one, like those Musketeer stories you read us back in Los Angeles."

"I see. So no matter what happens, you plan to stick together."

"No doubt," he said with a decisive nod that reminded me so much of my Joe.

"That is exactly what I hoped you would say, Zeus. Let me tell you why. If you venture out, first the boys lose their strong leader - you. Next they see you play semi-pro ball and want to join you and can't because they are too young. They might well give up. I think it's admirable that you have decided to wait until Posey is of age."

"Nothing admirable, Miss Beth, its family. We are nothing apart, but we are something really special together."

I dropped back in my chair as I exhaled. I knew I had done the right thing. I knew the bond the boys had built since they moved to Ooltawah was solid. Our conversation was the first time any of the boys had brought up Olivia's illness. None of the Los Angeles doctors could help her. I had watched medical announcements, and there was a doctor in New York who I thought might be able to treat her successfully. I knew that was the next thing I had to do – find medical help for Olivia.

I was lost in thought, and I was startled when Zeus leaned toward me and gave me a kiss on the cheek.

"Thank you, Miss Beth, for everything."

I knew I had gained the children's trust. My plan was working better than I had imagined.

Zeus left the room and headed for the bedroom he shared with Apollo, Midas, and Mercury.

It was a short rest. At five-thirty in the morning, Coach Tudor was at the front door. I had breakfast fixed for the lot of them. When Coach entered the kitchen, he was surprised to find all ten boys dressed and eating a hearty breakfast.

"I figured you boys would be sleeping in from yesterday's excitement."

"No, sir, Coach," Merc said as he chewed on grits, eggs, and bacon. "Yesterday is gone. We have to focus on today."

Zeus smiled, pleased with Mercury's answer. One by one, the boys had gotten baseball fever.

The next few days of practice were grueling. Bruises, scrapes, and cuts were common. Miss Eveline sat on the bottom bleacher waiting to bandage the next injury. Poseidon had the most wounds. Coach Tudor rewarded Posey with a pass on the twenty laps and ended practice at five in the afternoon.

Mayor Albright sent out his city engineer and a work crew to construct more bleachers, rest rooms, and a snack bar. He intended to charge the fans to repay the city for its investment.

Little did any of us know that all hell was about to break loose.

CHAPTER ELEVEN

Zeus was warming up on the mound at five o'clock the next morning. He looked around at all the bleachers, lights, snack bar, and the construction still under way. As he turned and surveyed the fence line, he noticed signs marking four hundred feet, five hundred feet and six and seven hundred feet. He was angry that the mayor was about to reveal to the world their stats. The center field distance signs were the last straw. Zeus threw his glove down on the pitcher's mound and stormed into the kitchen.

"Beth, you have do something about Mayor Albright. Have you seen what all he is doing to our ball field?"

I turned around and gave him a stern look. "First, Zeus, I am not Beth. I am Miss Beth."
"Yes, ma'am. I'm sorry. I was upset," he said, dropping his head.

"There is never an excuse to be rude, son. Your tone is unacceptable. Now, you march yourself out that door and try this again

Zeus bounced into the kitchen, smiling. He walked over to me as I stood at the stove cooking a huge breakfast of pancakes and sausage. He kissed me on the cheek.

"Good morning, Miss Beth. How are you this morning?"

I gave him a big smile. "Why, Zeus, I'm fine, and you?"

"Say, Miss Beth, have you noticed what our illustrious mayor has done to the ball field?"

"Why, no, I haven't, Zeus. Is there something you need to tell me about what the mayor is doing?"

"Yes, there is, as a matter of fact. Why our ole' mayor has fenced off our field and erected distance markers that indicate four hundred to seven hundred feet. Why, I think that's an infraction of our stats, Miss Beth."

"And what do you think we should do about it, Zeus?"

"Well, short of having him drawn and quartered, maybe we should consider taking the signs down."

"And why is that?" I had to struggle to keep from bursting out in laughter. I flipped the pancakes as I turned back to Zeus. He was sitting at the kitchen table, eating a sausage.

"Well, now, you see Miss Beth, one of the things we have going for us is nobody knows how far we hit. Those signs will take that away from us. It's a valuable asset that we just aren't quite ready to expose, you see."

I got serious because I knew this was an important issue for him.
"I do see your point, Zeus."

"Well then, Miss Beth, then perhaps I and the boys can fix up those signs."

"And by fixing up, you mean...."

"Sledgehammer, Miss Beth."

"You and the boys have my permission. But I think Coach should conduct the sledgehammer session."

"And, of course," he continued, "There's the matter of the fence. Now, just suppose some young kid, say Posey's age, wants to watch us play ball. If he has no money, he's left out. I don't think that's quite fair, do you?"

"Of course not. Every child who wants to watch you boys play ball should be allowed to do so. I think Coach may have a solution for that as well. Let's talk with him before we do anything rash." I burst out in laughter, and Zeus left the table to give me a hug.

"I saw what you were doing," he said. "You knew I let that mayor into my head, didn't you? You knew I cracked, and you had to straighten me out. Miss Beth, you are too much."

The boys came and went, tummies full of pancakes and sausage. I watched them out the kitchen window, and I knew Olivia was watching from upstairs.

At seven that morning I called the mayor and asked him to come over. I stressed it was a serious matter. He pulled his Cadillac into the long, dirt driveway about an hour later. Coach Tudor waited in the yard, and he followed me as I walked to the mayor's car.

"Morning, Mister Mayor," I said.

Coach nodded a greeting.

"And how are you good folks this morning?" The mayor was all smiles as he got out of his car.

"Come on up to the porch, Mister Mayor. I have orange juice, coffee, and hot homemade biscuits."

"Miss Beth, you are a woman after my own heart. You know I love those homemade biscuits of yours."

"Yes, I do, Mister Mayor." Coach, the mayor, and I settled on the porch with a plateful of biscuits, butter, and jelly, and hot cups of coffee. Coach watched the boys practice and waited for me to begin. The mayor was on his second biscuit when I got down to business.

"You know, Mister Mayor, we really appreciate your excitement about the boys."

"Why, thank you, Miss Beth. They are the biggest thing around these parts since the cow jumped over the moon. Those boys are about to put our fair city on the map."

"Yes, they are," Coach, said.

The mayor sat back and wiped his mouth.

"Now, you said we need to discuss some serious matters, Miss Beth. I let the world stop because of your call. Got lots to do, getting ready for Saturday's ballgame. How do you like the additions to your field?"

"Well, Mister Mayor, that's why I called, there seems to be some conflict here, and I thought I'd best point it out to you in person."
"Conflict?" the mayor said, looking a little indignant.

"Well, Mister Mayor, I don't think it's proper for city money to be spent on private property. Folks might get the wrong idea."

"Oh, yeah, that. Well, I got that all figured out. See, we charge admission and profit from the concessions, and we make that money back. The city is repaid, and no one is hurt. No harm in helping you folks out."

"Yes well, you see therein lies the rub. We don't need help. We aren't poor people, struggling to make ends meet. Now, if we needed your help, we aren't opposed to asking for it. Thing is, sir, you have violated our privacy. You are trying to make my boys a circus that will benefit your city. Now, I am not opposed to Ooltawah, which has been very good to us, to profit in some manner, but I assure you, it won't be like this."

The mayor had stuffed half a biscuit in his mouth while I was talking, and in his indignation, he sputtered and spewed biscuit crumbs all around his seat. "What are you talking about?" he demanded.

"We can start with that wooden fence," Coach said, letting his anger show.

"Well, I'm having that put into place so we can charge admission."

"No, Mister Mayor, we aren't," I told him, careful to keep my voice soft and polite.

"Aren't what?" he asked.

"Charging admission."

"But, Miss Beth, it only makes sense."

"For you, maybe, but for us the sensible thing is for anyone who wants to enjoy a good ballgame to come as they are and enjoy our hospitality. That doesn't include a cover charge."

The mayor flushed, but he kept his temper. "Well, what will you good people have me do?" he asked.

"First, Mister Mayor, you may want to consider speaking to us before you do anything on this property. Sending your engineer to measure how far the boys were hitting in the last game was just plain dumb. No, wait – putting up distance markers, now that is really, truly very dumb."

"But I don't get it. Those boys were hitting farther than major leaguers. I would think you would be proud of that."

"We're prouder than you can imagine, Mister Mayor. We just aren't prepared for the world to know their stats. I'll bet you, along with all the others that were here, didn't notice our boys running the bases better than most major leaguers, and no one had the chance to see those boys hurl a ball three hundred feet either. You get the word out that these boys are major league material at their ages; you could ruin their lives. I will not have those boys put in that position."

"How fast can they run the bases?" the mayor asked.

"Under twenty seconds," Coach, said proudly. "But, my friend, your ears are closed to what this lovely lady is telling you. They all have abilities that meet and exceed major leaguers. We've known that for some time. They are naturals. Not some of them; all of them. Ooltawah will get its due when the time comes, Mister Mayor. You are rushing the egg to hatch, sir. You can't do that. The boys have the abilities but not the maturity. They can't handle the stress at their ages. They need time to mature. In the meanwhile, we develop their skills."

"So you see, Mister Mayor," I explained, "while your intentions were good, your actions could be catastrophic for my boys. Now, we've decided we will play this Saturday's exhibition game. My boys will lose miserably. They will play like most kids their age. If you bet any money, you'd best put it on the men's all-star team."

It was the coach's turn to sputter. "We'll lose?"

"Yes," I said firmly. "If the boys win that game, there's no stopping the train. I'm not having it. They are too young."

Coach nodded, confused.

"Mister Mayor, I want the fence down today and the markers removed. Your Ooltawah glory will have to wait about three years. Posey is the youngest. I figure when he turns eighteen, the boys will be ready. Not before then. So I suggest you focus your energy on being re-elected, if you want credit for Ooltewah's finest ballplayers. Now I am done with this conversation. If there's anything you don't understand, ask now."

The mayor seemed dejected but resigned to my plan.

"You made yourself pretty clear. Three years, huh?"

"Yep, that's the plain fact as we sit here in God's sunshine," I said.
The mayor slowly got up and walked to his car. His step was a whole lot less confident than when he had arrived. He took his handkerchief out and wiped his baldhead. He shook his head, mumbling, got in his car, and drove away. Thirty minutes later, a work crew arrived to take down the fence and the markers.

The boys were disappointed. They wanted to sledgehammer it all.

Coach and I sat on the porch watching the work crew. Coach wasn't ready to throw Saturday's game.

"Miss Beth, you really think that's a good idea. I mean, the boys are just getting a bit of confidence. I was thinking...."

"Now, Harry, you're a good friend, but my mind's made up."

"Yes 'sum, but..."
"Harry, I tell you what: My Joe will be here tomorrow. You and I will talk to him. Whatever he says goes. Fair enough?"

"Yes 'sum," he said, "I can live with that," and he walked out to the field where the boys were practicing.

I heard him yelling something to Posey about line drives, but I wasn't paying attention. I was thinking about my Joe. He would arrive in the morning. It had been months since we'd seen each other. I was still terrified that he would see himself or his old love in the children's faces. But I wanted him to watch these boys play. They needed his guidance and advice.

I stood on the porch and listened to the boys chatter. I heard Eros shout, "Hey, Coach, when you going teach us to slide? That looks so cool on TV."

"Son, if you run fast enough, you don't need to slide," the coach shouted back, and the boys all laughed.

The boys were incredible athletes, I knew that, and I wasn't sure I was offering the right advice. I knew my Joe would have the right answer. He had lived the baseball life. No one knew baseball better than he did.

Joe won first place in the equestrian competition, but he told me later that all he could think about was seeing me again. I was petrified. What if he figures out the most dreaded secret?

CHAPTER TWELVE

I couldn't sleep, just thinking about my Joe coming for the week-end. So I got up early and fixed breakfast, and then waited on the porch. I saw the dust fly as the taxi came up the driveway, and I knew he was here! My heart was pounding. My Joe was finally here!

The taxi pulled up, and I ran to greet my husband as he swung open the car door. Joe tossed the driver a twenty and told him to keep the change. He grabbed his suitcase from the back seat, flung it on the ground, grabbed me, and held on tight. We held each other for a long, long time. Neither of us spoke.

The taxi driver, a boy from town named Randy, waited.

Joe finally noticed him. "Son, what are you waiting for?"

"I didn't want to be rude and throw dust all over the two of you," he said, but I knew what he really wanted was to spend time with my famous husband and eat some home cooking.

"Come on in. I have breakfast and coffee ready Randy," I said.

"Thank you, ma'am. Don't mind if I do." He jumped out of the taxi and headed for the house.

Joe and I looked at each other and laughed.

"What's with the ball field?" Joe asked as we followed the taxi driver in the house.

"It's a long, long story, Joe," I answered as I hugged my husband. By the time we got to the kitchen, Randy was already filling his plate with biscuits, ham and gravy.

"I hear tell your boys are about to break some records, ma'am," he said.

"Your boys?" Joe said, surprised.

"Eat, Randy, and stop talking." I laughed nervously.

"Your boys?" Joe repeated.

"It's a long story," I told him.

"Okay, I got the weekend. Will it take longer than that?"

I tried to think of a way to distract him. "First, tell me about your competition. How are the walkers?"

"Honey, they did great. The English club has asked me over. They want me to stud out three horses. All three draw a hundred grand a pop."

"That's wonderful. Have they told you how long you will be in England?"

"Six months, maybe less. Why?"

Before I realized what I was doing, I started to cry. Joe put his arms around me and waited in silence for me to tell him what was wrong.

"I have a mess here, Joe. I tried. I did my best, but I am at a loss."

"Yes 'sum you got yourself a mess, all right," Randy spoke up between bites of biscuit. "That mayor of ours is fit to be tied."

Joe looked amused. "You got the mayor mad at you, dear?"

"Oh, I'm sure he's pretty mad. But he is the least of my worries."

"Yes 'sum," Randy said, "I'd say that's about right. Mayor Albright will get past it all. Bigger worries are for sure."

"Who is this guy?" Joe asked.

"I'm your taxi driver, sir."

"Well, shouldn't you be driving your taxi? My wife and I are trying to have a conversation here."

"Oh, you two married? See, no one knew Miss Beth had a husband. Just a lot of boys."

"What?" Joe hollered. "That's the second time he said you got a lot of boys. Will you please tell me what's going on?"

"Randy, you made enough trouble. Finish your breakfast and hit the road. Oh, and when you are telling the whole town I'm married, be sure to say my boys are out of wedlock," I snapped.

"Now, hold on, Miss Beth," Randy protested, looking aggrieved. "I ain't one for rumors."
"This whole town thrives on rumors. Now, before I say what I'm thinking, you best leave."

"Yes 'sum," Randy said as he put two biscuits in his jacket pocket and headed out the door.

I turned my attention to my husband. "I know there's a lot to explain, Joe. Let's walk down by the lake. I had a park bench put there when I knew you were coming. It's so peaceful there, Joe. The story I have to tell you may break your heart. I'm just not real sure how you will take all of this."

We walked outside and through the meadow to the new park bench. We sat for a few moments, watching the ducks. Joe gave me time to collect my thoughts. It was time for him to hear the truth, but not the whole truth, I decided.
I turned to Joe. "Dear, do you recall the first time you took me to the airport to fly here?"

"Yes, I do."

"Well, in the misses' will, my instructions were to watch over a child, an illegitimate child from a family that she knew. That's why I came here, to check on her."

"I see. Go on."

“Well she grew up, married, and had a passel of kids.”

“How many is a passel?”

“Twelve.”

“Damn, she did have a passel, didn’t she?” Joe said with a laugh.

“Yes, but problems happened between her and her husband.”

“I’m not surprised.”

“I visited them, and what I found was disgusting. The kids were rude, loud, hateful, and out of control."

“Where was the mother?”

“Joe, she is ill, mentally ill. So I have pitched in to help. I got them moved here from Los Angeles, had a ballpark built for those ten boys to burn off energy.”

"Ten boys?" Joe whistled to show his astonishment.

"Yes, dear. Ten. What has happened since has created a lot of controversy. I hired a retired major league coach to organize them. You may have heard of him, Harry Tudor."

"Yes, he was an excellent coach in the bigs."

"Well, he is now an extended family member. He practically lives here."

"Why?"

"Well, um, the boys have shown remarkable talent in baseball."

"That's good. How many of the ten?"

"All of them. Every one of them, from the oldest to the youngest."

"Well, it sounds like to me you've got everything under control."

"Well, not really, dear. You see we have an aggressive mayor. He invited the Chattanooga firemen baseball team in to play against the boys."

"That doesn't sound fair. How old are the boys?"

"Fifteen through twenty."

"That's awful young. And they played against men?"

"Yes, they did, dear. Zeus, he's the oldest, pitched a no hitter."

Joe raised his eyebrows. "That's impressive."

"The boys went through the batting order, three times, and the men's team gave up."

"You're telling me the boys beat the men?"

"Slaughtered is a better word, dear. Now the Chattanooga mayor is all mad because his men's team lost to boys, and the Ooltawah mayor is mad at me because I told him no fences and distance markers. See, the Ooltawah mayor took it upon himself to add more bleachers, bathrooms, concessions, and he built a wooden fence around our ballpark, so he can charge admission. He says so he can repay the city for its expenses. I told him yesterday to take the fence down and removed the distance markers."

"I understand why you didn't want the fence to keep people out, but what about the markers? What's the problem, there?"

"Well, it tells the world the boys' stats. We aren't ready for the world to know that they hit over six hundred feet."

And I told him how far they could throw and how fast they could run.
I could tell Joe was having a hard time believing me, but he was trying to give me the benefit of the doubt.
"Well, it sounds to me as though the problems will sort themselves out. I think maybe measuring and timing must be the problem."

"Well, that's not all, Joe. The Chattanooga mayor is really angry. He has gone on a citywide all-star hunt. He says the boys are going down. Except I know they won't, and there's my problem. Scouts from everywhere will split the boys up; most are of age to play. They will feel abandoned. Zeus says he isn't leaving his brothers. But I just don't know."

"When is their next practice and when is the all-star game? I'll stick around for them."

"They have already started practice. That's why I brought you out here, so I could talk to you and not be distracted. The all-star game is tomorrow afternoon. Thousands of people will converge here. It's just amazing."

"Okay, let's go see these boys and see what's what. Just relax, dear. There's nothing here that can't be fixed." Joe pulled me close and whispered in my ear. "I missed you. I love you so much." We walked back to the house, holding hands.

CHAPTER THIRTEEN

Joe sat in the mayor's covered seat and watched the boys. Zeus hurled a fastball dead center in the strike zone; Merc was batting and connected, sending the ball over six hundred feet. Joe stood up and looked around to see if anyone else saw what that kid did. He was astounded.

Eros came up to bat, braced himself, and waited for what he knew was going to be a hot one. Joe lost sight of the pitched ball; the next thing he knew, it was sailing more than six hundred feet.

Joe watched them pitch, hit, and run bases. He stood up and walked over to some cardboard boxes that just arrived. He opened a box that held a speed gun. He took it out and stood behind the backdrop. As Hermie got up to bat, Zeus pitched a fastball, Joe squeezed the trigger. The speed gun registered one hundred and three miles per hour.

"That's impossible," Joe said out loud. Coach looked over, recognized him, and smiled.

Zeus's next pitch Joe clocked at a fraction over one hundred and three. "Damn," he whispered.

After a while, Joe dropped the speed gun, and Coach figured it was time for a chat. Coach sent the boys to run their twenty laps. Joe was standing still, dumbfounded.

"Hello, Joe. How's the world treating one of America's greatest?"

"Hello, Harry," Joe mumbled.

"Pretty impressive, huh?"

"Impossible is what it is. The speed gun is broken."

"No, Joe, it's brand new. You took it out of the box. I watched you."

"No one can pitch like that, especially a kid."

"I know. That's what's so exciting, Joe. I got 'em running the bases at fourteen and below and hitting high line drives over six hundred. Our outfielders can lob a ball into the catcher's mitt at four hundred feet every time, and with a little more work, I think I can get the pitcher up to a hundred and five miles per hour."

"He's already there, Harry. I clocked him at a hundred and five exactly. I also clocked one kid running the bases at thirteen flat."

Harry glowed with pride. "That's my boys," he said. "So are we going win tomorrow? Miss Beth says you will determine if we lie down and let the all-stars beat us or not. She thinks the boys will get corrupted or something playing so young."

"It's not that part she's worried about. She's worried about splitting them up. We talked about that. She never mentioned the possibility of laying down in tomorrow's game, though. I've never done that in my life. Can't understand why these boys should."

Joe stretched out the kinks in his back and clapped Coach on the shoulder.

"Well, I've had enough excitement for today, Harry. I'm hungry. Let's get us something to eat."

The two men walked into the house and sat down at the kitchen table, waiting for me to finish cooking.

"Who named those kids?" Joe asked, causing me and Coach to chuckle.

"Olivia, their mother named them. She has a thing for Greek mythology. Their father is Greek."

"Where is their father?" Joe asked. I told him the story of the couple's marriage and divorce. When I had finished, Mr. Joe said, in a no-nonsense tone, "Call him – right now."

I got Eric on the line and handed the phone to Joe.

"We need to discuss your sons," he said without preamble.

"Are they in trouble again?" Eric asked.

"No, sir. It's more serious than that. Listen, are you familiar with Chattanooga, Tennessee?" Without waiting for an answer, Joe continued. "Look, you fly into Chattanooga. I'll make the arrangements. Be at the ticket counter at three this afternoon."

"Now, hold on," Eric protested.

"If you love your family, you be on that airplane. I'll meet you at the airport and pick you up," Joe said flatly and hung up.

I hugged Joe. "Oh, thank you, Joe. You put that man in his place, just fine. The boys will be excited to see their dad."

"Let's let his arrival be a surprise. Besides, if he doesn't show up, the boys will be disappointed. No need in putting them through that."

The men ate ham biscuits, and then Coach stood up to leave. "We have plenty daylight left. We need to practice," he said.

"Harry," Joe said. "The boys play hard ball tomorrow. No lying down. I won't have it." Coach grinned with relief and headed for the door.

"Thank you, Joe," I said. "I just feel like I made such a mess of things. I'm so glad you are here."

"Seems to me you saved this family from chaos, dear," he answered. "From what I've heard from you and Coach, it seems like those boys were headed for disaster."

"Thank you, Joe. You always put things into perspective for me."
"Dear, you need no one to clear up matters for you. You do well on your own. Now tell me about Olivia."

"She's seriously ill, Joe. She sits at her bedroom window and watches her boys play ball all day long. She seldom eats, and she hardly ever comes downstairs. It's just like when she was a kid. The doctors can't seem to help. There's a doctor in New York who sounds promising to me. I had considered flying her to New York."

"Let's do it," he said. He stretched and yawned. "Well, if you don't mind, I'm taking a nap. Eric Jacobi will be here this evening - at least, I hope he will."

Joe pulled me close and gave me a passionate kiss, a hint, I knew, of things to come that evening. I giggled. Even at our age, we couldn't get enough of each other, and we had been apart way too long.

When he left me, I glanced outside at the girls. Artemis and Demeter were playing with their dolls on the porch. They seldom left the porch. Much like their mother, they were reserved and quiet. I knew I would be taking the girls to the doctor with their mother.

CHAPTER FOURTEEN

That evening, Joe met Eric at the airport. Joe told me later Eric went pale when he realized who he had talked to on the phone. He had not expected to be met at the airport by one of the world's most famous men.

Eric stood in astonishment for a full minute before finally offering Joe his hand. "I had no idea with whom I was speaking on the phone," he told Joe. "You are my all-time hero."

On the taxi ride back home, Joe filled Eric in on the situation with his family. He told Eric about my plan to take Olivia to New York to see a doctor. Then Joe talked about the boys. "The boys are fine. In fact, astonishing is a better word. Did you know they are all skilled baseball players? Every one of your boys is a superior ballplayer, down to the youngest."

Joe and Eric talked about their skill, which surprised their father, and Joe rebuked Eric for letting the boys "run wild." "It's no wonder they were heading in the wrong direction," he said.

"Well, my second marriage ended about three years ago," Eric told Joe. "She wasn't someone I loved, but someone I met after the divorce. Olivia has always had my heart."
When the talk returned to the boys, Joe told Eric about the upcoming game. "I imagine, from what they've told me, this all-star team will be pretty dang tough. My wife wanted them to throw the game. You know, lie down, and let the all-star team have a win. I refused."
"Why would she want to do that?"

"Well, it's the ages of your boys. Posey is fifteen. That's awful young to be thrown in the limelight. Zeus has already been offered semi-pro, but turned it down. He won't leave his brothers. He says all for one and one for all. It's a noble idea, but I'm not so sure a smart one."

Eric nodded. "I played semi-pro in my early twenties. I had to decide between swimming and baseball. I chose swimming because my swim times were good, and, well, I had a good swim coach."

"Then you understand what your boys have accomplished at such a young age?"

Eric nodded again. "But there's a problem," he said. "They don't listen to me. They still have bad feelings towards me. They think I abandoned them. Truth is, I couldn't live with Olivia any longer. She got way too nuts for me."

Joe frowned. "And you just left the children with a woman who is mentally ill? Well, maybe that's why they are angry with you. Not because you left them, but because you left them in an unstable environment."

"Yeah, you're probably right. I just couldn't take it any longer. I was stupid."

"Well, my friend, you are about to take a lot, or disappear again. Those boys have a bundle of problems in front of them."

"Just how did you get involved with my boys?"

"Apparently, my wife nursed Olivia when she was just a child. Beth kept up with her. She visited Olivia and the boys about eight months ago in Los Angeles and found nothing but grief. Angry boys, in trouble, the house a wreck, and Olivia seldom, if ever, left her bedroom. The boys were just wild as animals, desperate for attention from anyone, including the law."

Eric hung his head. "I don't know what to say."

"Try saying I'm sorry to each and every child."

When Joe and Eric got home, I was sitting on the porch rocking. Olivia was upstairs in her rocker, and the children had gone into town with Coach. Eric went upstairs to Olivia and stayed for more than an hour. Joe and I sat on the porch and rocked next to each other, holding hands. The sunset was breathtaking,

and we could hear the crickets and locusts sing.
When the children got home, Eric was waiting. The boys were chattering about their trip into town, and then fell silent one by one as they noticed their father on the porch. Artemis and Demeter ran to their father and hugged him. The boys followed the girls up on the porch and surrounded Eric. He cried, and so did most of the boys.

Joe and I left the porch and went for a walk. Coach joined us.
We could hear them talking excitedly to their father, and then we heard Eric apologize to each of his children for his absence.

"Dad, you don't have to do this," one of the boys protested.

"Yes, I do, son. Please allow me this. I am sorry I hurt you by leaving. You are all special, and I love you. I never stop thinking about you."

The boys told me later what happened next. The kids all turned around at the same time to see their mother standing on the porch. The evening breeze swept through her beautiful hair.

"Mommy's up!" Artemis yelled. The kids gathered around her, hugging her and holding her hands, smoothing her hair, and telling her how pretty she looked. The family took the first step to becoming a family again that night. They talked for hours. Olivia smiled as her ex-husband took her hand into his. Eric's cell phone kept ringing, but he ignored it.

When the children finally went to bed, Olivia and Eric were left on the porch alone. Joe and I went around to the back door, so as not to disturb them, and went up to bed. Olivia and her ex-husband had some catching up to do, and Joe and I had some catching up of our own in mind.

CHAPTER FIFTEEN

Coach Tudor gave the boys the next morning off from practice. Joe and I spent the morning relaxing. The house was quiet, and I thought the boys had decided to sleep in. I had no idea they took the truck into town to swim at the town's public pool.

Joe and I went out to the porch and sat on the creaking porch swing. Around ten, Eric came down, poured a cup of coffee, and joined us on the porch. For a long time, no one spoke. Eric seemed troubled.

"Miss Beth," he said at last, looking over the ball field, "what made you take on my boys?"

Here it was again - the question that wouldn't go away, the secret that, sooner or later, must be told. Joe sat quiet. He, too, wanted to hear the answer to that question. I felt cornered. But I didn't have to answer after all. We saw the family's pickup come flying down the driveway toward the house. The three of us knew instantly something was wrong.

Zeus slammed the driver's door and ran around to the bed of the truck. Vulcan was lying down, and his brothers were crowded around him.

"Miss Beth," Zeus hollered, "Vulcan hurt his arm!"

Thank God it wasn't worse, I thought. An injured arm I could deal with.
The boys tried to tell the story all at once, but we finally got all but Vulcan to quiet down. He told us he had been roughhousing in the pool with his brothers and had slammed his arm against the pool's concrete wall.

Eric loaded Vulcan and Zeus into the pickup again, and they raced away to a hospital in Chattanooga. The news wasn't bad, but it was tragic in Vulcan's mind because of the upcoming game. The doctor said he would have to rest and let it heal for five or six days.

Coach fussed at Zeus for taking the boys swimming, but Eric took his son's side. "Look, Coach, the boys had an accident. It's that simple. Now lay off Zeus. He sees what happened and feels bad enough. What we need to do is focus on the game."

Coach nodded and clapped Posey on the back. "Looks like it's up to you son. You up for it?"

My little Posey looked a little nervous, but he didn't hesitate. "Yes, sir, Coach," he barked.

I watched out the kitchen window as cars and trucks pulled up. There must have been four hundred people an hour before the game. The concession stand was humming with business, and I could smell the hamburgers and hot dogs cooking. Blankets were spread, picnic style, all over the grounds. People sat on car hoods and kids sat in the back of pickups. Those who couldn't afford to buy food and drink brought coolers of cold drinks and homemade sandwiches. Those who couldn't park nearby parked up the road and trudged into the yard.

Coach took the brothers, all fresh in their uniforms, down by the meadow. He wanted to

warm them up away from the crowd's view. Vulcan's arm was in a sling, and I could tell from his face, he was unhappy and embarrassed.
I watched as Coach put the boys through their paces. Eric and Joe stayed on the porch, amazed at the crowd. There must have been thousands there that day. No one was prepared for such a turnout, least of all Posey. His eyes were big as saucers.

Zeus and Posey walked away from the coach and their brothers. We all knew why.

"Look, Posey," I heard Zeus say, "If you aren't up to this, we can call this whole thing off. It's no big deal."

"It is a big deal," Posey answered. "I mean, I knew I would eventually get called in, just not like this. I am ready to play, that isn't what bothers me."

"Well, what is it, then?"

Posey looked down at the grass swaying in the breeze. His answer was a long time coming. Zeus waited, with his arm around his brother. Posey looked like he might cry.

"Zeus," he finally said, "Dad has been gone for three years. I'm afraid if I screw up in the ballgame, he will disappear again. I can't let that happen. We are finally coming back together as a family. You boys will hate me if I drive him away. I'll hate myself, too."

"You think that Dad is here to watch you play ball, and if you don't do well, he will leave again? What am I going to do with you, little brother? Let me explain a few things. First, Dad left us, not because of you or any of the kids. Mom's illness drove him away. He is here because he loves us all, not because of what we can and can't do. Look, you learned to play ball as well as any of us. You have no idea how proud I am of you. Look, man, you took the practice abuse as well as any of us and hung in there. You hit as well as any of us, you run just as fast, can throw just as far. You have skills that I only wish I had at your age.

Can you imagine what kind of ballplayer you will be in three or four more years?"

"You think?" Posey said, looking a little less scared.

"There's no doubt, little brother. It's a gift. Don't you know why all those folks came here today?"

"Yes, to watch you guys play ball."

"No, silly. They are here to see kids, your age, do the impossible. You, little brother, are the star on our team. Don't you remember what Mom told us when we were smaller? She always said, "Snowmen fall from heaven unassembled."

"I remember," Posey said.

"Look at yourself, little brother, you are assembled. Now let's go kick some ass!"

Coach noticed Eric on the porch. He led his team up to the porch and, one by one, the boys hugged their father. Eric sat in his rocking chair and whispered to each, "I am so proud of you." As Posey, the last in line, reached for his father, he stopped and stared at the screen door. It was partly open. The sun shone brightly on a light yellow dress. Olivia's hair was brushed and beautiful, her smile warm and loving. She hugged her boys as they gathered around her.

"Now, I want you boys to show your dad your stuff," she said. "I am so proud of all my young men. Zeus, you lead the way."

The boys formed a line, arranged, as usual, by age. Zeus looked back at his mom, and she winked at him. Posey stared at his dad. Eric gave him a thumbs-up. The boys walked out onto the field, taking their positions. Vulcan sat on the bench, head down.

Our town's mayor, anxious when he saw Vulcan's sling, whispered something to his wife. Mayor Wilson, seated next to Mayor Albright, strained to hear.

"So, Albright, looks as though one of your boys is injured."

"Oh, it's minor," Albright, said quickly. "He's fine. You'll see."

"No, sir," Mayor Wilson said, punching Albright jovially on the arm, "my bank account will see – it'll see a large deposit in about two hours."

"Yes, well, I wouldn't be counting my money till the game is over," Mayor Albright snapped. Albright's wife placed a calming hand over her husband's and told both men to hush.

The bus pulled in. It was lumberjack time. Mayor Wilson stood and applauded for his team. They were huge men, and they looked determined. The firemen's humiliation in the last game had reached legendary status. It was pretty obvious these men had no intention of suffering the same fate. They came ready to win. Their set jaws and grim faces made me

uneasy for my boys. Joe held my hand and squeezed it lightly.
The two mayors flipped a coin. The all-stars went to bat first. The crowd hushed. Thousands of spectators from five counties went silent as Albright threw out the first ball.

Joe settled back in his rocker, next to me, and waited with everyone else. He looked so handsome with his shiny, silvery hair. Even in the rocker, he sat straight and proud. I knew I had been truly blessed to have him in my life. I wondered if he had seen any resemblance to himself among the brothers. Posey, in particular, looked a lot like Joe.
Mayor Tudor had hired four umpires from the Chattanooga Choo Choos' league. He wanted the game clean and fair, no matter what. Besides, his winnings from Mayor Wilson would reimburse him nicely, with interest, he was sure. The city money he spent on the farm would be more than made back from today's concessions. Most people probably would have brought their own food, had they known the mayor was charging six bucks for a hot dog and seven for a burger. Cokes were two

dollars and fifty cents. He wanted to sell beer, but I put my foot down on that one. No alcoholic beverages around my boys, I told him.

Ump Johnson, the plate ump, stepped forward with an arm raised to the pitcher and yelled, "Play ball!"

Zeus gave Posey a quick wave. Posey nodded. The boys told me later how there were feeling as play began.

Zeus started his wind-up; leg lifted off the mound, and released his first pitch. He expected to hear the ball thud into Apollo's glove, but instead, he heard the bat connect with the ball. The ball sailed to left field. It was way over Posey's head and coming at him with a vengeance. Posey ran as fast as he could toward the barbed wire fence.

He kept saying to himself, "I'm assembled. I'm assembled." As he turned, he saw the ball dropping. He knew he had made a mistake when he took his eye off the ball. His stomach churned. His heart pounded. Eric and Joe stood up from their rockers. They yelled in unison, "Come on, Posey… catch it!"

Zeus covered his face with his glove. It was the first hit an opposing player had ever gotten and now he had placed his baby brother in a dead-out run trying to beat the ball's flight.

The crowd stood, hushed. Mayor Albright loudly sucked in his breath. Mayor Wilson smiled as he leaned over to his wife and said out loud, "No way."

Posey was out of breath, heart pounding, as he reached as far and as high as his arms would let him. He felt his feet leave the ground as he lunged upwards. The sun made his eyes water. He heard a scream from center field: "Watch out for the fence! The fence!" The crowd held its breath.

CHAPTER SIXTEEN

Posey's arm snapped back from the force of the ball, his feet thumped soundly back to earth, and his arm swung in a complete backwards circle. He opened his clenched eyes and smiled. Ice cream cone, he thought. He was holding the rocket hurled at him by the tip of his glove. He thrust his arm up, showing the ball. The crowd went into an uproar. Zeus jumped and twisted in midair. Tuneboy shouted from third base, "Now, that's playing serious ball!"

Eric and Joe high-fived each other as I sat, unable to move. What I had just watched, I would have never believed had I not seen it for myself. A boy become a young man, an athlete of the highest caliber. He had turned a home run into just another stat in the out column. The hitter trudged back to the dugout from second base looking dejected.

Posey hurled the ball into his brother's glove from four hundred feet away. Apollo turned to the crowd and showed the ball. The crowd cheered.

Coach had to sit down in the dugout. He hadn't had that much excitement since the World Series he coached in '92. Olivia smiled. She knew her Posey had done well. She had no idea just how talented he was, but the semi-pro scouts among the spectators were duly impressed. Turned out, the best was yet to come.

Zeus called a time-out. He called his teammates together. They all wanted to give Posey his due. As they slapped Posey on the back and gave him hugs, the crowd added to the celebration. Everybody started chanting Posey's name.

Zeus looked proudest of all. "Boy, you ain't just assembled, but you are well-assembled," he told Posey. "Now let's kick some ass. I got past my first pitch; you got past your first play. There ain't going to be any more hits. I'm about to show these boys they can't hit off me. Now let's get to it!" Zeus held out his right hand. The brothers stacked and broke on Zeus's command. The brothers claimed their territory, knowing Zeus was about to pour on the heat.

Joe told me later he sensed what was about to happen. He went in search of the speed gun. He wanted to know just how fast Zeus's pitches were. Joe didn't notice there was three other speed guns pointed at home plate.

Joe sat on the ground behind the cage, ready to record history. The next batter came out of warm-up. He was a giant of a man - six feet, six inches, two hundred and sixty pounds. He had won last year in all the competitions in Chattanooga for the batter who could hit the farthest. He must have known scouts were watching and his career was on the line.

Zeus wound up and focused on Apollo's glove. He let loose the ball, and it whizzed past the batter into the strike zone. Joe looked at the gun - one hundred and three miles per hour!

The ump stood stunned for a second and then called a strike.
Apollo called time and ran to the dugout.

"Coach, Zeus is tearing up my hand. I need something, anything. If he keeps moving the ball that hard, I can't catch it." Joe walked over and showed Coach the ball's speed.

"Damn!" said the coach.

Joe kicked off his two hundred dollar loafers and pulled out the gel insole. He put the insole inside the glove. As Apollo headed back to home plate pulling his mask down, Coach asked Joe, "You think that will help?"

"Hell, I have no idea. But I sure wouldn't want to be catching a ball whizzing at a hundred and three miles per hour. I would take any relief I could get. Let's hope it works."

Everyone took their places again. The count was one and zero.
Zeus rocked back and fired off a perfect down-the-center heater. Joe's gun registered it as one

hundred three. The batter couldn't see the ball. He knew it was coming because he watched Zeus as he did his windup. He never swung. "Strike two!" the umpired bellowed.

Major Albright jumped out of his chair waving his hands in the air. Mayor Wilson began to realize he might have lost the five grand he bet.

As Zeus lined himself up for the third pitch, he heard his brothers chattering all around him. "Come on, big brother, show him you walk the walk," Achilles hollered. Tuneboy shouted, "Zeus is the best, the strongest, and the ugliest."
Zeus smiled, and then grew deadly serious as he looked at the batter. He hurled the ball, grunting as he let it go.
Joe's speed gun clocked it at one hundred four miles per hour.
The ump shouted, "Strike three, you're out!"

Blue, gooey liquid ran down Apollo's arm. He looked up at the ump, which called a time-out. The ump wanted to know what the blue stuff was, and he wanted to get a look at the speed gun. He had never called a game where he couldn't see the ball. He was frustrated, and a bit cranky.

Ump Williams walked toward Joe. He stopped dead in his tracks and pointed when he recognized the man with the speed gun. "Say, mister, aren't you..."

"Yes I am, ump," Joe replied.

The ump wanted to shake Joe's hand. "America's greatest! Well, I'll be hanged. You know these boys?"

"Yes, they are close friends."

"What is that kid putting on your speed gun?" the ump asked. Joe knew he wouldn't believe him, so he handed over the gun.

Ump Williams's eyes bugged out and his mouth dropped open. He looked from the speed gun to Joe and back again.

“I know,” Joe said. “That blue, gooey stuff is the lining from my shoes.” Joe took off both shoes to show the lining missing in the right one. “I gave it to Apollo. The power of Zeus’s pitches was more than the boy could take.”

“Damn!” the ump said, heading back to home plate. “I thought my eyesight was failing me.”

The ump bent over Apollo and gave Zeus the sign. “Play ball!” he yelled.

The third batter was nicknamed Ox. He was an ex-marine. He had played minor league for two years before he screwed up a knee. His power hadn’t diminished, but a runner was always used for this power hitter. Apollo heard the grinding of this man’s batting gloves as they got a grip on the bat.
Zeus wound up and released. Apollo’s glove puffed a small cloud of dust. Joe clocked it at one hundred and one.

On the next pitch, Zeus threw a hundred and two. Joe knew Zeus was backing off. He thought maybe Zeus was getting tired. He asked Coach to take a time-out. Joe walked out onto the field and the crowd roared. Their standing ovation showed they had not forgotten him. Joe waved.

"You all right?" Joe asked Zeus.

"Sure, I'm fine."

"Your arm strong?"

Zeus nodded.

"Then why are you backing off?"

"I'm hurting Apollo's hand. I can see him wince."

"Son, you never back off. Ever. Your brother can handle whatever you toss. Now I know you have the strength to throw harder. That's exactly what I want you to do."

"Why?

"Because you can, son. Because you can." Joe stared hard into Zeus's eyes. "No man ever gets where he wants to be by easing up. You either give it all you got or leave the mound. Your brothers all know you backed off. They see you do it, and they think it's okay. It's never okay to give less than your best. Now you hurl that ball for all its worth, or I will ask Coach to pull you off the field." Joe turned and walked away.

Zeus knew Joe was right. His brothers were watching his every move, and he also knew they took their lead from him.

Joe pointed the speed gun while Zeus wound up. Zeus released the ball with a grunt that came from way down. The ball hit Apollo's glove with a force that rocked him onto his backside. The speed gun registered one hundred and five.

"I knew it!" Joe whispered to himself.

The brothers ran off the field, throwing their gloves at Zeus. The crowd stood and cheered.

The commotion lasted five minutes. Joe was at the dugout as the boys returned. He hugged Zeus and handed him the speed gun. "I'm proud of you, son," he said.

The brothers pulled the gun away and stared at the reading. "Geeze!" one said. "Man oh man," said another. Posey, the last to take the gun, handed it to his father. Eric's jaw dropped, and his eyes widened. His smile told the boys he was proud. I stood off the side of the dugout, crying. I watched father and sons bond.

Coach broke up the celebration. "Okay, boys, its stick time," he said. "Anybody that gets less than a high line drive down the middle gets a kick in the butt from me and everybody out there watching this game. Now get your heads back where they belong. We can celebrate after we beat these gorillas."

Zeus came out of the dugout, crossed his legs at his ankles, and bent down to stretch. He heard a sexy voice from the bleachers say, "Man, you have a sexy butt." He looked around but couldn't tell where the voice came from. He shook it off and focused.

As he walked towards the batter's box, he could barely see the ump. The catcher was a mountain of a man. As Zeus got nearer, the catcher growled at him. The ump gave the catcher a swift kick in the rear, a brave thing to do since the catcher was twice his size.

Zeus took the batter's stance. He recognized the pitcher, and his resolve deepened. He knew thousands of people were watching. He had a job to do. He wanted a piece of the first pitch. He knew how important it was to take this pitcher down.

The pitcher let go, and Zeus took a deep breath and smashed the ball into center field. It was a high, long drive that no one could possibly catch. The city engineer hurried over to Mayor Albright. He whispered in an agitated voice, loud enough for Mayor Wilson to hear, "That was more than seven hundred feet, sir."

Both men stood and applauded. The crowd went crazy. This time the scouts timed Zeus's base run. He could have relished the moment, but he chose to run his best, just like Coach had trained all the boys to do. He rounded the bases in a little over twelve seconds, just one second under the major league record. The scouts compared stopwatches. None of them could quite believe what they were seeing.

The crowd gave Zeus a standing ovation. The Coach made him walk out of the dugout. He tipped his hat as the crowd roared. He heard that sexy voice calling to him again, but he still couldn't identify the woman in the bleachers. He walked back into the dugout, looking over his shoulder.

Apollo took his place in the batter's box. The first pitch was wild and outside, but the second was exactly what Apollo wanted: a heater down the center. He connected with a thwack as the ball sailed high over center field and fell just short of Zeus's hit.

The engineer estimated the hit at just less than six hundred and fifty-four feet. He was out of breath by the time he got to the mayor, and he didn't bother whispering. He breathlessly announced how far he estimated the ball had gone. Both men stood and applauded Apollo. He was already back to home plate and entering the dugout when they stood to acknowledge his hit. Coach made Apollo go back out and tip his baseball cap.

One by one, the boys came to bat. Each one hit the ball more than six hundred feet.
When it was Posey's turn to bat, the opposing team had fire in their eyes. Perhaps they hoped that the youngest brother was also the weakest. Coach told Posey to take the first two pitches. Everyone in the dugout knew Posey was about to be pitched some trash. Posey was alert and ready. He, too, recognized the opposing pitcher. Posey had seen the man on TV many times.

The first two pitches were low and inside. The count was against Posey, but he held his ground. He focused on the third pitch. He braced himself, just as he had seen Zeus do. He tightened his grip as the ball came hurling at him. He reached deep down inside, found what he needed, and connected with a vengeance. The ball flew higher and faster than any ball hit that day. All the brothers came out of the dugout to watch its flight. Posey dropped his bat and ran. He couldn't feel his legs; he didn't see the crowd; he didn't think about anything but touching home plate. He knew he had a home run, but he ran hard just the same.

The scouts clocked him at twelve seconds flat. They gaped at each other, not sure whether to believe their eyes. "Shit!" said one, and the other two nodded.
The engineer ran to the mayor, completely out of breath and barely able to talk. The mayor waited impatiently until the engineer recovered. "About seven hundred and fifteen feet, sir," he finally announced.

The all-stars caved. Nine to nothing was just too embarrassing. They didn't want a thirty-run lead score. They admitted defeat.

The brothers took the field near the pitcher's mound with their coach on their shoulders.

They carried him to the mayor's box and dumped him off. "Mayor, here is the hero of Ooltawah," Zeus said. "This man drove us like cattle in a stampede. Our wins are his wins. If you have a medal, it goes on this man's chest."

Mayor Albright could barely hear Zeus over the noise in the stands, but he took Coach's arm and raised it for the spectators to see. He promised a city council proclamation making Coach Tudor Ooltewah's coach of the decade. Coach told me later it was at that moment that he decided to come out of retirement and open training camps for young ballplayers.

The celebration went on for hours. Joe, Eric, Olivia, and I had all retreated to the back yard, where barbecue was cooking in an open pit. Coach invited the umps to stay for barbecue, and the scouts invited themselves.

The boys stayed close to their father. Joe and I kept our distance, wanting to give them privacy. Coach Tudor spent his time reliving the game with anybody who would listen. The scouts ate and listened to the boy's chatter.

Mayor Wilson and Mayor Albright argued for hours after the game about the bet. Wilson had hired Andy Mendex, a semi-pro player, to pitch for the all-star team. Mayor Albright thought he should have to pay a “fine” for cheating. Mayor Wilson thought he should pay nothing at all because, he declared, the game was somehow “rigged.” Eventually Mayor Albright got his five thousand dollars.

The evening was cool as the sun set on the far side of the farmhouse. Olivia sat quietly in an oversized, white, wooden chair near her husband. The boys couldn’t keep their hands off their parents. The Jacobi family had never been happier. Hermes and Demeter sat close to their mother.

Zeus caught me staring at him. He smiled at me with that crooked smile. I smiled back. Joe watched the exchange. He still had no idea why his wife was so caught up in this family. Zeus walked over to me and put his arms around me. The brothers followed Zeus. I dropped my head and smiled. Zeus kissed me lightly on the cheek, and I blushed.

"Joe, sir, let me tell you what your wife means to us," Zeus began. The boys all moved in closer to me. Each had to touch an arm or a hand. Posey took my right hand and held it tightly in his.

"She saved our lives. She took us out of a place where our lives were out of control. She faked being a housekeeper, persuaded our mother to sell our home, and moved us here. I don't know how she knew baseball, maybe that was your influence, but your Miss Beth is our hero. She is Memaw Beth to us. The best grandmother that any kid could have."

I couldn't help but cry. I was so overwhelmed by the boys and their love. Grandmother? He called me their grandmother? The circumstances that led up to this day, no one could know but me. I couldn't tell a soul. Or could I? Those lawyers, Keyes and Ottoman, were no longer a concern. I heard Keyes died of a heart attack and Ottoman's kids placed him in a nursing home two or three years ago. What did I have to be afraid of? A neurotic woman who died decades ago? Or was I afraid to tell the man I loved with all my heart.

There was no logical reason to keep my secret any longer. Joe was a wonderful man who had lived his seventy-two years without children. His family sat around him, and he didn't know. I was the only outsider and the only person who knew the truth. This family of champions deserved to know. I stood and cleared my throat.

"Everyone listen. I have something to say."

CHAPTER SEVENTEEN

Miss Eveline came out the back door with a tray of chicken thighs and legs for the grill. She heard my little announcement, put the tray down, and placed both hands on her hips.

"Girl, if you are about to open up, now is not the time." Eveline nodded toward the scouts and umps.

"I waited for this moment far too many years to stop you, but you best be thinking before you let your mouth loose." Eveline swung around to the tray of meat. She busied herself placing the chicken on the grill. Joe sat quietly. He knew there was more to this than met the eye. But he knew me. He knew, given the right circumstances, I would tell him everything. This was not the right time. There were strangers in our midst.

"Oh, I'm just being silly," I said and sat back down.

"Well, gentlemen," Joe said as he eased out of his lawn chair, "How is that barbecue?"

"Mighty good, Joe. Thank you for having us," Henry Tolliver, a scout, said around a mouthful of the succulent meat. Everybody else nodded, too busy chewing to talk.

"Well, fellows, as you can tell, the family has business to conduct."

"Oh, yes, sir, we got that impression," one of the scouts said. "We won't hold up a family meeting here. We are prepared to make an offer for Zeus, Apollo Hermes, Achilles, and Neptune."

"An offer?" Joe boomed.

"Yes, sir," Tolliver spoke up. "We can offer all of them a fifty thousand dollar signing bonus, and we are authorized to offer one million for Zeus on a two-year contract and three hundred thousand on the others for a one-year contract."

Midas and Merc slapped each other on the shoulder.

"Now, hold on there, boys. These gentlemen were just leaving."

"Joe, I need to take an answer back to management. With the stats we have on these boys, we will probably lose our jobs if we don't seal this deal. This time tomorrow, every scout in America will be after your boys."

"Well, they aren't my boys, first off, but I think I am close enough that I can answer your offer as no deal."

"We can go higher, Joe," one of the scouts said.

"Go as high as you like; these boys aren't for sale. There will be no piecemeal here. It's the package or nothing, and the package costs twenty million dollars. Take that back to your management," Joe said as he sauntered back to his lawn chair and eased back into it.

"Yes, sir, we will take that back, but I don't think...."

"Son, you probably haven't given this any thought. We saw what those boys did on the field today. They are primed and can take the pendant from any major league club. You can tell your management that, too. Now, say your goodbyes and off with you."

In unison, the three scouts said thank you and goodbye. They tipped their hats and piled into a car. The trail of dust they left behind told us those three guys were ready to leave.

The two umps walked over to Joe. "Sir, that was the fanciest business we've ever seen," Williams said. "Aside from watching these boys play ball, that was the highlight of our day. Management at the Choo Choos is prepared to pay exactly what you asked. They just wanted the guys cheaper."

"These young men aren't old enough, just yet."

"Yes, sir, I understand what you're saying, but five years ago, they drafted a sixteen-year-old, and Posey is already on the other side of fifteen. Yes, sir, they are old enough. Just something to think about, sir. I'm sure you will do what's right by these fine young men. I do want to say if you ever need an ump, it will be my pleasure working with these gentlemen. I've never umpired a better game than today. Some players are like spoiled brats. These young men have manners and class, sir."

The two umps said their goodbyes and headed back to Chattanooga.
Coach stood and began his farewells, but Olivia began talking. Coach wasn't going to be rude, so he sat quietly and listened.

"I remember faintly - so faintly that sometimes I think it must have been a dream - but there was this young woman. She was so pretty. She used to come to my room at Miss Eveline's and read to me. It was a mythology book." She looked around at her children. "That's where I got all your names, from that book." She stared off into the distance. "I recall this woman cutting my hair until I was almost bald."

The boys looked at each other and shrugged, wondering what she was getting at.

"My hair was so tangled and matted down to my scalp. Then one day, she got it all cut out and could run a brush through my hair. I've brushed it with that silver brush she gave me, ever since."

"That's nice, dear," Eric said not understanding what she was talking about.

"No, no. Let her finish," I said. "Go ahead, Olivia, tell us what it is you want to say."

"Well, inside the book was a book marker with a picture of a man. On the back was a lot of writing about his height, weight, and stuff, but at the bottom was something that has stuck with me all these years."

"That was a baseball card, Olivia. What did it say?" I asked, taking her right hand and holding it gently.

"There was handwriting on it that said 'To a wonderful person in my life.' It was signed 'Joe.' I held that picture and its autograph close to my heart every night. I cried myself to sleep at night, begging him to come get me. I use to pretend he was my daddy."

Tears welled up, blurring my vision. I looked around at this wonderful family and I knew, no matter who was listening, no matter how many newspapers picked up the story, I didn't care. I knelt in front of Olivia, wobbling a little. Joe was behind me in a flash to steady me.

"Why are you crying?" he asked.

"Because, Joe, that man in that picture IS her daddy."

No one moved and no one spoke. A pin falling into the grass could have been heard. They exchanged confused looks, and then looked at me expectantly.

Joe broke the silence. “Now, honey, maybe you should start from the beginning. It must be quite a story.”

I rose from my place in front of Olivia and sat atop the picnic table. Joe came over and sat close to my side. I knew I had to do this. I had to be strong. I couldn’t look at him.

Coach stood. “Maybe I need to leave now,” he said.

“No, Coach, you are as much a part of this family as any of us,” I said. “I want you to stay. You will understand better what you’re dealing with here.” My mouth was dry. My tears would not stop. I thought a moment, and then began my story, knowing I could lose the love of my life for hiding such a sinister secret.

I told them first about my childhood and my decision to leave home. I told them about arriving in Hollywood and my search for employment.

"Late that first evening, I had an interview with a woman who lived in a fine home. She was beautiful and a famous movie star."

I told them about the nine years I lived with her, about the marriages and many miscarriages. But it was Olivia's birth that they had to know about.

"In her seventh month, she somehow made herself have that baby," I said. "When I went into the room, she was laying there in a pool of blood, holding the tiniest baby I've ever seen. I thought it was dead. It wasn't moving. I bundled my misses and the baby up and drove to the emergency room. I was shocked to find her two attorneys were there. She gave that baby up for adoption. She was as cool as a winter breeze. I know it had to be the medication she was taking to control her moods."

Four years later, that beautiful woman died, I told them. No one ever really determined how or why. There was a lot of mystery surrounding her death.

"She left me a great deal of money, and in her will, she asked that I look after her baby girl." I paused, and then said softly, "That baby girl was Olivia."

Miss Eveline started to cry. Joe rubbed my arm as I continued.

"Olivia, it was I who read to you and cut your hair. I had to, just to get it where you could brush it. I cried when I saw that silver brush on your dresser upstairs. I loved reading to you. The only book I could find at Miss Eveline's house that I thought you might enjoy was a book on Greek mythology. I didn't care what it was about. All I cared about was getting through to you."

"Lord, that book belonged to my great-granddaddy," Miss Eveline blubbered to Coach.

I took a deep breath and went on. "Joe had given me that autographed baseball card the day before I left Los Angeles. Olivia, look at me. That man in the picture IS your father! That's his autograph!"

Joe shot up from his seat, shock registering on his face. "You mean…"

"Yes, Joe, Olivia is your daughter! That's why we are here. We're looking after my misses' baby girl."

"Hold on there," Posey said. "If Mother's dad is Joe, then he has to be my grandpa!"

"Yes, Posey, that's right. Joe is your grandfather." I answered the questions slowly and deliberately. I wanted everyone to understand.

Joe walked over to Olivia's chair. He knelt in front of her. I had never seen his hands tremble until this moment. He reached out, took Olivia's frail right hand into his own, and kissed it gently.

"Olivia, I am in the man in the picture. I am here to protect you and make you safe. I see your mother's eyes and her face in yours. She was a beautiful woman, Olivia. I'm sorry you didn't have a mother and daddy growing up. I didn't know until this very moment."

Olivia took her dad's hand and kissed it.

"Well, I'll be," Coach, shouted. "Hell, no wonder these kids have bucket loads of talent. Their grandpa is the one and only Joe. Add in Olivia and an Olympic swimmer, and this is what you end up with: dynamite in all ages!"

Everyone laughed, and it helped ease the tension.

Olivia looked at Joe and said, "You have no idea how many nights I prayed you would come save me, like the gods in the book saved the mortals they loved. I prayed to your picture."

"Well, my dear, you no longer need that picture or the autograph; you have me. I'm here, and I'm never leaving your side again."

"Joe, I am sorry I hid this from you. I was afraid if I told you I would lose you forever."

"You can't get rid of me. You protected my family. Maybe I should be angry for not knowing but Beth, I love you and I've learned everything you do is for a purpose. Whatever happened in the past is left where it belongs. I have a family and we have a future. All of us. Together. If there's any anger it's overshadowed by your love for me and Olivia and her family.

"What about your horses? You have that trip planned."

"Hell with them. The trainer can take over. I'm staying with my daughter and her family. I have a family, Olivia," he said, and I saw to my amazement that he was crying. He looked up at me and smiled through his tears. "We have a family, Memaw Beth!"

CHAPTER EIGHTEEN

No one stirred early the next day except me. The boys were exhausted. Joe was drained. Coach ended up sleeping on the daybed on the back screened-in porch.

I was up early, making breakfast and getting packed. The flight for New York would leave at noon. Miss Eveline had agreed to stay with the boys. Eric, Joe, and I were taking Olivia and the girls to see the new doctor who specialized in depression and other mental illnesses.

We arrived in New York on Sunday afternoon. The appointments were scheduled for Monday morning. I didn't sleep all night.

As we entered the office of Doctor Wiseman, the receptionist met us and took Olivia and the girls to other rooms. There was a reason for our separation. Olivia was taken to a waiting room and left alone. She sat in the middle of the room and rocked. The two girls were separated, too, and each sat alone in a room and rocked their baby dolls. A team of doctors watched them closely. Cameras documented their behavior. Doctor Wiseman went into Olivia's room and spoke to her gently. Olivia's response was barely audible.

The evaluations lasted all day. Late that afternoon, a nurse called Joe, Eric, and me into a conference room. Five doctors sat around a long table. An older doctor, Jeremy King, did most of the talking.

"Mister Jacobi," he said, "your wife and daughters suffer from acute depression. We think maybe there is a genetic connection. One thing we are most definitely sure of is the three females in your family suffer from Bipolar disorder, or, as it's more commonly known, manic depression. It's caused by a chemical imbalance that can be treated with medication."

His words frightened me. "Doctor, I know I'm really ignorant about such matters, but I have to ask: Are you saying they have to be sedated?"

"Not at all," he answered. "We will start them on Lithium and Thorazine and adjust their dosages until it fits their needs. There may be side effects, such as drowsiness, and the agitation and depression may not go away immediately. But we'll find the proper dosage, and their symptoms will improve."

Eric spoke up. "How long, do you think, until we really see improvement?"

"We generally can tell from the start which way to go with the dosage, so my guess is maybe two weeks."

The doctor explained that Olivia and the girls would stay at the medical facility until the doctors had determined the dosage and were satisfied there would be no serious side effects.

"Now, let me tell you before you ask the next question: No, you may not stay. We prefer you not take a hotel nearby and needlessly tire yourselves. Go home. We will call you when our work here is done. We have a high rate of success. You have some of the best medical help in the world for your family members."

"But, Doctor…" Joe protested.

"Please, sir," the doctor interrupted. "You asked for our help, and all I ask is that you trust our judgment and allow us to give them the help they need. Frankly, if you insist on staying or visiting during therapy, we can't help them. It's imperative that patients rely on themselves to get better. Family gets in the way."

"We are just so close, it is difficult to turn loose," I said.

"Yes, ma'am, we all understand. But the fact is, you've done everything for Mrs. Jacobi and these girls. I'd be willing to bet that when Mrs. Jacobi wouldn't come sit at the dinner table, you took her food to her and coaxed her to eat. We know you meant well, but that won't do."

Joe stood. "Doctors, we'll leave them in your hands."

The doctors all stood. The meeting was over. I wanted to cry out, "Wait, I'm not finished! I want to know more! I don't want to leave my baby girl and her baby girls alone with strangers." But Eric and Joe hustled me into a taxi. I wept, and Joe patted my hand.
We flew back to Chattanooga the next day. The boys met our taxi as we pulled into the yard. They were looking for Olivia, Artemis, and Demeter. Eric explained that their mother and sisters were in a hospital, but they would be home soon. It was a solemn gathering around the dinner table that evening. No one spoke, and we picked at our food.

After dinner, Eric, Joe, and I sat rocking on the porch, talking about baseball, and the good ol' days when Joe was at the top of his game. He was paid big money in the forties - nearly two hundred dollars a month. By today's standards, that would be about two thousand a month. Zeus alone would command millions in the majors someday.

The evening breeze felt good. The cold months were ahead, and even with the Cumberland Mountains blocking most of the snow and ice, it could be frigid in February. The evenings cooled off quickly now, and the crickets sang their song less and less in the evenings.

Posey and Zeus tossed a ball back and forth in front of the porch, as Eric and Joe talked about their own glory days. Miss Eveline and I were tired. Housework and feeding a small army every day can wear a body down, I thought. Then I realized how Southern that expression was, "wear a body down." I was starting to sound like Miss Eveline, and so were the boys. They had all begun to talk with heavy Southern drawls. They were happy in their new environment and wanted to fit in.

At dark, the phone rang. Joe answered it and came back after a five-minute conversation.

"Who was it, dear?" I asked.

"The owner of the Choo Choos. He's on his way over here. He wants to discuss the boys."

"Well, dear, don't you think that's Eric's job?"

"No, ma'am, I don't. They are my grandsons. I can speak for 'em."

"Spoken like a true grandpa," Eric said, and he laughed and slapped hands with Joe.
I bristled.

"You boys are messing with me, aren't you? You know something you ain't telling."

"Now, missy, let's not start accusing people of keeping secrets. You held a secret for dang near thirty-five years."

"Dang near? Is this Southern thing rubbing off on you Joe?"

"Yes 'sum, it is," Joe said, bowing low like an old-fashioned Southern gentleman.

"Well, I suppose when you're ready to tell me, I'll find out."

Miss Eveline threw back her head and laughed. Her ample belly jiggled under her cotton shift, and her eyes danced.

"Beth, ol' girl, those boys throwing that ball around out there are millionaires."

"Have they signed contracts to play ball?"

"Nope, I've left them everything in my will," Joe told me. "They ain't got to play ball for anyone. They are what we used to call independently wealthy."

"I see. So if they are millionaires, then maybe their grandma is, too?"

"Sweet thing, you became a millionaire when you married me."

"I see. Then why have I had to use my own money all these years?"

"I was saving it all for my grandsons. I got a lot of them, you know."

"I see. And what about your granddaughters?

"Them too, of course."

"You crotchety old man," I said, taking a swipe at his arm. "Okay, so tell me why those men are coming over."

"To discuss the boys."

"Do they want to sign them or what?"

"Not sure. Depends."

I lost all patience and raised my voice. "Stop cat-and-moussing me, Joe. I'm serious. Tell me what they want."

"They're offering a pile of money. They want to scoop them up before any other team has a chance."

"Look, Joe, we can't sign any contracts."

"And why not?"
"Because I said so."

Joe looked like he didn't know whether to laugh or get mad.
Miss Eveline stood and dusted off her apron. "You two sound like three-year-olds. Just listen to yourselves."

I wasn't ready to let it go. "You two boys have something cooked up. I know it."

"We do, indeed," Eric said, his hands clasped behind his head, looking quite satisfied with himself.

"Well, let's see," I said, "you told the scouts twenty million, and they are still talking. You don't mean you're asking for more."

"Yes 'sum, lots more," Eric, said.

"I won't have it, Joe. You hear me? I won't have it." I could tell my angry outburst took Joe by surprise. He wasn't used to defiance from me.

"And what would you have us do, my sweets, let those boys play for nothing?"

"Exactly!" I yelled as I stomped off, slamming the screen door behind me.

Twenty minutes later, Eric, Joe, and three men in business suits sat huddled in earnest discussion. I tried listening but couldn't make out what they were saying. I had an idea. The screen door squeaked as I pushed it open with a tray of iced tea. I offered our company a glass first, then Eric. When I got to Joe, I stuck my tongue out at him. Eric saw it and jumped, spilling his tea across his white shirt.

"You need to see to that, Eric," I said politely as I shooed him from his rocker, plopped down in his seat, and handed him the tray. The amount on the table was eighty million dollars for two years.

"Gentlemen, I'm sorry if these two have wasted your time. My boys aren't playing for no eighty million dollars. No way. Uh uh. Nope."

"But, ma'am, we were nearing an agreement," the most polished of the three protested.

"No agreement can be consummated without my approval. Seems I arrived just in time," I said as I rocked. "Now, let's talk serious baseball."

The men looked at each other and rolled their eyes.

"Oh, I see. I'm a woman, and women can't talk business. Is that what you're thinking? Well, let me explain something to you: Those boys are where they are today because of me. No one else, certainly not the two men on this porch. So I decide their future. It's just that simple. You either deal with me, or I take my boys elsewhere."

Joe looked at me with amazement, and perhaps a little respect.. He had never seen me like this. I had never imagined I could be like this. But my boys' futures were at stake, and nothing else mattered at the moment.

The three men looked over at Joe, hoping maybe he would make me hush. But Joe surprised us all. "She's right, boys. And when she makes up her mind, she won't budge." He waved his hand at me. "Go ahead, dear, make the deal."

I sat up and looked those men in the eye. "Okay, this is what I want for the boys. I want you to change your gate from eighteen dollars to eight. I want children under fifteen to get in free. I want five hundred seats a game set aside for orphans and children of single parents. I want concessions rolled back to 1955 prices. I want this game of baseball to be given back to the kids of America. You meet my demands and you got my boys."

"But, madam," sputtered one of the men, "we can't afford to pay the boys millions and roll prices back. We will go broke!"

"You aren't listening. I want my boys paid 1955 wages. Not a dime more."
The three men in suits sputtered more as Eric, Joe, and Miss Eveline laughed and clapped.

"That's the deal, take it or leave it," I snapped. " As long as you treat my boy's right, and as long as the youngest is too young for the majors, they can play for you. I say you have about eighteen months to make the most of it. Now you go back to your plush offices and put a pencil to what I'm proposing. If you can't figure out how to turn it into a windfall for your organization, my boys don't need to be playing for men with no vision."

I stood, held out my hand to shake theirs, and said, "Gentlemen, I believe you have work to do."

Their jabbering, sounding near hysteria, as they got into their limo and drove off. The dust trail was a small one. I've seen bigger and better. There was one brewing on the porch a lot bigger.

The boys had been hiding at the corner of the porch, listening to every word. As the men drove off in their limo, the boys came out, whooping and hollering.

CHAPTER NINETEEN

Zeus was the only one not jumping. I saw him standing off by himself.

"You had all this planned, didn't you, Miss Beth?" he asked.

"No, Zeus, not all of it. I knew you boys had super potential, and I knew I had to get you out of Los Angeles. The rest has just happened as we went along. Does it upset you, what I told those fellas?"

"Upset? Not hardly. I couldn't have said it any better. I've watch kids get millions and ruin their lives. I know you are protecting us, but I think your mission is way deeper than that. Say, Posey, stop acting like a wild man and come talk to Miss Beth and me. Posey is the brains of this outfit. He sees stuff no one else can." Zeus sat on the edge of the porch. "Okay, Posey, you heard all of what Miss Beth had to say, now educate me and your brothers."

Eric and Joe sat still in their rockers. They wanted to be educated, too.

"Well, Miss Beth loves us. She wouldn't let those men take advantage of us. She could have taken them to the cleaners. I mean she could have gotten a lot of money for our contracts. Instead she chose for us to make a few bucks, have a lot of fun, and stay upright and clean."

"That's true, Posey, but there's more, isn't there?" Zeus prodded.

"Well, Miss Beth knows if we get a lot of money, we could become independent and nasty, like most of the ballplayers. You know the ones that want to charge for their autographs and play ball for the money. She wants us to keep it real, as they say back in Los Angeles. She is keeping us grounded, Zeus."

Posey thought for a minute and added, "She's keeping us together as a family. But you know what else? She is taking the game back to the kids. She is making sure kids that can't afford a ticket get to go. With her rules, that means the stadium will be filled with kids our age. Miss Beth wants us to show those kids that, with a lot of hard work, they can develop into whatever they choose to be. We will be heroes to kids our age."

I stood and applauded. Posey was right on target.

"No one could have said it any better," I told him. "Any baseball player who can't be bothered to give a kid, any kid, an autograph without charging him or brushing him off doesn't deserve admiration. I'll not have you boys turn into that kind of player, an adult brat who demands his own way. You are more than that. You are better than that. I plan to keep you that way, as long as I am around."

The porch was quiet. Eric and Joe sat, dumbfounded.

In two weeks, Eric, Joe, and I flew up to pick up Olivia and the girls.
Olivia was sitting on the side of her hospital bed when we came in. Her head was down. For a minute, I thought nothing had changed. But then I saw she was trying to undo her necklace clasp. When she saw us, she beamed. She looked beautiful. I heard Eric sigh. The woman he married was back. He took her in his arms and kissed her, and he cried.
The nurse brought in the two girls. Artemis, now thirteen, and Demeter, twelve, looked cheerful for the first time since I had met them. They ran to their mother.

Artemis said it best. "Mommy, I can see you! I'm not in a fog anymore."

I insisted on finding the doctor to thank him personally.

"Thank you, Doctor, for giving those lovely girls back to us. Olivia looks radiant, something I thought I would never see. You truly do work miracles." I gave him a hug, taking him by surprise, I think.

Back in Tennessee, a homecoming celebration was being planned, and we had so much to celebrate. Olivia had so much to come back to: a father she never knew, a loving husband, and twelve kids who adored her.

The homecoming was incredible. The whole town of Ooltawah must have turned out. Demeter counted all the barbecue grills going all at once, twenty-five of them, she said.

Olivia was like a beautiful butterfly. She floated from one group to another, introducing me as her mother. My heart swelled at each introduction. I had gone from housekeeper to mother and memaw Beth. Joe never left my side. We relished watching our granddaughters find friends their age.

As the celebration came to an end, I noticed Miss Eveline and Coach sitting together in the front porch swing. I couldn't help but giggle. Coach had fallen in love – or maybe he was just in love with her incredible Southern cooking. That man sure had an appetite. My best guess was he loved her and her cooking; I could tell by the look on his face and swell of his stomach.

Eric and Olivia remarried three days later in the back yard. Only family members, Coach, and Miss Eveline were invited. I was honored to be bride's maid. Zeus gave the bride away. It was the first time I had ever seen Zeus cry.

Two days later, the Choo Choo big wigs were back on our porch. Eric and Joe sat and listened. The men spoke directly to me, the little woman.
They agreed to my terms. They wanted the boys to take on a team the Choo Choos had never been able to beat.

The stadium was always packed when the boys played, and happy children made up much of the crowd. I allowed the boys to endorse one product. I set two conditions: They must use the product they were to endorse, and all the money they made went to Doctor King's research department in New York. The boys chose to endorse Wheaties.

Their grandpa had graced the box decades before.

The boys all loved giving autographs. They knew of one very special autograph that was closely connected to their family. They never turned a child away.
The good mayor kept insisting they move up to the majors.

"They might", I told him, "or they might not. It depends on the gate prices and the housekeeper."

The End

11768714R00157

Made in the USA
Monee, IL
16 September 2019